...any advice?

by Tucker Shaw and Fiona Gibb
illustrations by Sara Schwartz

AlloyBooks

To Susan O., who reminded me how to listen.—TS
To all my ex-boyfriends, especially the ones who still ask me for advice.—FG

Acknowledgments: Big thanks to Alloy.com brass Matt Diamond, Jim Johnson, and Sam Gradess. We wouldn't be here without you guys. Props to Angie Maximo, Lauren Goodman, Deb Goldstein, and the rest of the Alloy crew for all their input and writing. Shoutout to the 17th Street crew: Les Morgenstein, Ann Brashares, Josh Bank, Cecily von Ziegesar, Russell Gordon, Lauren Monchik, and everyone else up there at the end of that scary elevator ride. Many thanks to Sara Schwartz for her rad illustrations. Aren't they rad? Thanks y'all.

All love to Susan Kaplow for creating this opportunity.

And most of all, love to everyone in the Alloy.com community. Thanks to you, we have something to write about.

ALLOY BOOKS
Published by the Penguin Group
Penguin Putnam Books for Young Readers,
345 Hudson Street, New York, New York 10014, U.S.A.
Penguin Books Ltd, 27 Wrights Lane, London W8 5TZ, England
Penguin Books Australia Ltd, Ringwood, Victoria, Australia
Penguin Books Canada Ltd, 10 Alcorn Avenue, Toronto, Ontario, Canada M4V 3B2
Penguin Books (N.Z.) Ltd, 182-190 Wairau Road, Auckland 10, New Zealand

Penguin Books Ltd, Registered Offices: Harmondsworth, Middlesex, England

Published by Puffin Books,
a division of Penguin Putnam Books for Young Readers, 2000

10 9 8 7 6 5 4 3 2 1

Interior illustrations by saraschwartz.com

Produced by 17th Street Productions,
an Alloy Online, Inc. company
33 West 17th Street
New York, NY 10011

ISBN 0-14-130921-0

Printed in the United States of America

contents

Sign-on

As the advice columnists for Alloy.com, we get a few hundred e-mails every day, asking for advice. And we do our best to come up with solutions to your problems, or give you some love, or back you up.

Sometimes that means we get to play broken-heart doctor. Sometimes we get to play sex columnist. Sometimes guidance counselor. And sometimes we have to slap you upside the head with a down-and-dirty reality check.

When we answer your questions, we always try to put ourselves in your place. Because no matter how many best-friend breakups, relationship meltdowns, or parental misunderstandings there are in the universe, when it's happening to you, no other problem in the world feels as big or important as the one you're stressing over.

Thing is, any problem you're dealing with is yours and only yours. We can try to break it down for you, and everyone else can throw in their point of view (and they do!), but at the end of the day no one—not your friends, not your family, not us—can tell you what to do. It's up to you.

But know this: You're not alone.

Need proof? Read on.

Peace,

Tucker and Fiona

I wish I was your size.
Then maybe Mike would ask me out.
Well I feel like I'm too tall -n- skinny
Gee, I feel so short & chunky lately.
Me too.
Chill chicas! All sizes rock!
Big is B-U-T FUL!

your body

Okay, you hate your body. You think you're too fat. Too skinny. Too freckly. Whatever.

And really, how can any of us avoid feeling physically inadequate when we're constantly bombarded by images of how we're supposed to look? Like those superskinny chicks in fabulous clothes on the covers of all the magazines.

Well, here's the deal: Unless you're a model, chances are, you're not gonna look like a model. Ever. No matter how many hours you spend at the gym. Or if you get a nose job. Or breast implants.

And you know what? If you and Tyra Banks were friends, she'd probably always be saying stuff to you like, "I hate my forehead," or "I wish I had your hair." Because models aren't perfect, either. That's what airbrushing is all about.

Fiona

am I too fat for a boyfriend?

Q. Dear Fiona,

I've been seriously bummed lately. I recently asked a guy out and he said no. I think it may be because of how I look. See, I'm kind of fat—like a size 16. I think I'm a good person, with a lot of cool qualities. But sometimes I feel like I'm never going to have a boyfriend because I'm not skinny. I have a lot of guy friends—but I've never gone out with anyone, and I'm 15. And even if I did go out with someone, I'm not sure I'd feel comfortable fooling around. It makes me really, really depressed.

What should I do?

—Not a supermodel

A. Hey, Not,

First of all, the average female model weighs 23 percent less than the average woman, and her body proportions are totally different, too. So it's unrealistic for you to compare yourself to them. The truth is, unless you were born that way, nothing you do is gonna make you morph into Rebecca Romijn-Stamos. And you shouldn't want to, either.

Second, are you sure this guy turned you down because of your weight? You shouldn't just assume that. Maybe there was some other reason he wasn't interested—like he doesn't want to date anyone, he likes someone else, or maybe he thinks of you as

Imperfections make someone

just a friend. And as much as that still bites, you can't let it bum you out. Because everyone gets dissed once in a while. You have to learn to not take it too personally, though. And most important, you have to not let it affect how you see yourself.

It sounds to me like you're a good person with a lot to offer. Deep down inside, you already know that. And sure, some guys may not give you a chance because you're not a size 6. But do you want to be with someone that shallow? I wouldn't.

So what do you do? It may be hard, but you have to hang in there. Trust me, you'll find someone special. One day the right guy is going to see just how cool you are. You'll feel totally comfortable around him. And he won't care what size jeans you wear. (In fact, he may like the fact that you're not a stick.)

But if you are unhappy or uncomfortable with your body, keep in mind that there are things you can do to make yourself look and feel better. I'm not talking drastic, starvation stuff—just simple things like getting more exercise and trying to eat healthier. Trust me, those little changes can give your self-esteem a major boost.

Take care,

Fiona

Coco <<Girl, if you feel this strongly about it, go on a diet. But don't do it for the boys–do it for yourself.>>

Vivien <<I'm a size 2 and I model. I don't have a boyfriend, and the guy I like isn't attracted to me. So it's not all about size and looks.>>

perfect to me. —Fred Durst of Limp Bizkit

what do guys think is hot?

Q. Dear Tucker,

What are guys really looking for in a girl? I know looks do matter. Do guys really care about chest size? Do they care about you being skinny? My guy friend said that guys think being really skinny is attractive.

–Curious

A. Dear Curious,

Sure, girls' looks do matter to guys. Just the way guys' looks matter to girls. Some guys care about chest size a lot. Some guys don't. Some guys think superskinny girls are hot. Some guys don't. Some guys like blondes. Some guys don't. I mean, think about it. You and your friends have different tastes in boys, right? Same deal with guys—they all have different tastes.

"Yeah, right," you're saying. Fair enough. I mean, it's obvious that guys spend a lot of time chasing "hot" girls—usually skinny ones with big boobs. But here's a big secret for you: The biggest reason they're doing it is because they think they should—it's what all the other guys are doing.

See, most guys are insecure about their own personal tastes and attractions. Just like most people are insecure about their taste in clothes or haircuts—they follow trends rather than do their own thing. Same with guys and girls. Since advertising and movies and magazines tell us that skinny girls with big boobs are "hot," we try to act accordingly. Just like when everyone decided cargo pants were "hot," we all went out and bought some. Not to compare girls to jeans or anything, but you know what I mean.

It's a stigma to have a pretty face and a good body. Like you're

The Power of Suggestion

Harvard psychiatrist Anne Becker linked the 1995 introduction of American television to the Pacific island of Fiji with subsequent dramatic changes in the body image attitudes of Fijian girls. Fijian people traditionally embraced larger, robust body types, but in 1998 roughly three in four Fijian teen girls said they felt fat, and 15 percent of girls reported vomiting to control their weight. "I never expected two thousand years of tradition to be washed away by a couple of years of [the TV show Beverly Hills] 90210,*" Becker said.*

Most guys don't make the effort or spend the time to really get to know those "hot" girls. We tend to get stuck on their looks, and very few guys look deeper. Which, if you think about it, isn't at all fair to those girls.

Anyway, there's one thing that's pretty much common across the board: In the long run, guys like girls who are themselves. Guys can't deal with fake girls. (Just like girls can't deal with fake guys. Come to think of it, fake people are pretty horrible to deal with.) Trust me: If you spend all your time trying to be something different, to fit someone else's definition of "hot," you'll be one lonely girl.

Be yourself.

Tucker

Lindy <<Girls don't have to be skinny to look hot 'cause different guys have different tastes.>>

not allowed to have everything . . . ! —Naomi Campbell

I can't lose weight being healthy

Q. Dear Fiona,

I want to lose weight! My friends are on that don't-eat-one-thing-no-matter-how-horrible-you-feel diet, and I'm on the cut-back-on-junk-food-and-exercise diet. But it's not working!! They're losing weight and I'm not, but I feel good and they're always sick. So how can I lose weight and feel good about myself?

–Detesting Dieting

A. Dear Detesting,

Some ways of losing weight—like your friends' scary starvation tactics—are seriously bad for you. They can cause lifelong health problems, ranging from eating disorders like anorexia to heart arrhythmias.

Crash dieting is not only really unhealthy, it's also not a permanent solution. The majority of people who lose weight that way end up gaining it back—and a lot of times they put on even more pounds than they shed in the first place. I know it may not seem like it right now, but you're taking a more sensible approach than your friends are. They're going for the quick fix

You've got to learn to like yourself first.

when in this case slow and steady wins the race. Because the only way to change your body is to change your lifestyle. Which means less Burger King and more basketball or whatever kind of physical activity you're into. But before you go any further with your diet, talk to your parents and doctor. They can make sure that what you're doing is healthy—and they may even be able to help you out.

Good luck,

Fiona

Yolama: <<Do you really want to be anorexic? It's disgusting to look like a chicken. Do sports that will build muscles and make you look good and feel great.>>

(Not So) Model Figures

- *More than half of all American women—about 65 million—wear sizes 14 to 24.*
- *At the turn of the century the ideal feminine figure—the Gibson girl (created by artist Charles Dana Gibson)—had bust-waist-hip measurements of 38-24-45.*
- *Brooke Shields, who has modeled since she was a baby, admitted that she's been dieting since age 8, when she "decided to give up soda pop and pizza."*
- *Glamour's "The Secret Life of Models" reported that fewer than 5 percent of supermodels have a stick of butter in their refrigerators.*
- *A generation ago the average model weighed 8 percent less than the average woman; now she weighs 23 percent less.*
- *Sex symbol Marilyn Monroe was a size 14.*

I'm a little screwed up, but I'm beautiful. —Steve McQueen

all she thinks about is her weight!

Q. Tucker,

Dude, I'm starting to get really annoyed with my girlfriend. We've been going out for a few months now, but lately all she talks about is how much she weighs and stuff. She's not fat at all, so why is she always freaking out about gaining pounds? It's getting really boring.

—Acorn

A. Acorn,

That can be annoying. Sadly, we live in a world that tells girls they have to be skinny—I mean model skinny—to be accepted. But the thing is, it's not true. And while girls are going crazy worrying about their weight, they don't realize that guys don't care nearly as much as girls think they do.

It sounds like your girlfriend has a little problem . . . but guess what? You can help.

First, stop being annoyed for a second and think about where she's coming from. Then give her some love. Tell her straight up that you think she looks awesome and that you wouldn't have her any other way. In fact, if you keep letting her know, maybe she'll change the way she acts. Or maybe she won't. If she has a serious eating disorder, you're not going to cure her—she needs treatment. But no matter what, a lot of positive vibes sure can't hurt. So let her know how beautiful you think she is just the way she is.

Later,

Tucker

Weigh this

According to the U.S. Public Health Service:

- *One-third of all girls in grades 9 through 12 think they are overweight.*
- *Sixty percent say they are trying to lose weight.*
- *Nearly half say they skip meals to control their weight.*

Jarmi <<I know you're annoyed, but whatever you do, don't start fights with her about this. If she feels threatened, she'll only worry about it more.>>

of a life-long romance. —Oscar Wilde

I'm bulimic

Q. Dear Fiona,

A couple of months ago I got really frustrated that I wasn't losing enough weight on this diet I was on. So I started throwing up after I ate once in a while. I know you're not supposed to do that, but I was really desperate. Now things have kind of gotten out of hand, and I'm doing it all the time. I can't stop. Is what I'm doing really so bad?

Help me,
–Scared

A. Hey, Scared,

There's no way around it—forcing yourself to puke after eating is bulimia, a very serious eating disorder. And yes, what you're doing is really bad for you—not only mentally, but physically, too. But it sounds like you already know that.

Let me just say that while you may feel okay right now, this habit is taking a toll on your body. Bulimia can cause major, irreversible damage to your lungs (food particles get trapped in your lungs and irritate them), kidneys (throwing up drains you of vital body fluids), heart (you're at risk for arrhythmias—irregular heartbeats), and more. In severe cases bulimia can cause death.

The condition also wreaks havoc on your looks—ironically, since that's what you were trying to change in the first place. Bulimia can give you bloodshot eyes, a puffy face, and gnarly teeth (stomach acid erodes tooth enamel).

The bottom line is that this is a very serious problem, and you need to get help right away. Talk to someone you trust and

Is it too much to ask that women be spared the daily struggle ask them to help you, and while you're at it, call your doctor to get referrals to local support groups and doctors in your area.

This is too major to go through alone, so get help now.

Good luck,

Fiona

OandH <<Personally, I'd rather be fat but otherwise healthy than skinny and stuck with a burnt-away esophagus, a screwed-up stomach, and missing teeth.>>

See p. 170 for help lines.

I'm very hairy

Q. Hey, Fiona,

I have this problem. Body hair. I know everybody has it, but I have too much! Especially on my arms. What makes it worse is that it's dark—so it's more noticeable. I'm really stressing out because swimsuit season is coming up, and I'm afraid to put one on! I was wondering if there was any permanent way of getting rid of it?

Please help!
Thanks,
–Embarrassed

A. Hey, Embarrassed,

Yeah, there's a permanent method of hair removal called electrolysis. It's superexpensive and time-consuming, and word on the street is that it can be painful. (Hello—it involves needles!) So I wouldn't really recommend it. Especially because I'm sure your body hair issue is a lot less major than you think. Everyone is really self-conscious about some aspect of their appearance. And everybody has parts of themselves that they don't like. Big ears. Frizzy hair. Flabby thighs. Whatever. The trick is practicing damage control on what you can—and learning to deal with and accept the rest.

I wish I was taller. I probably look taller

So you may want to think about trying a depilatory cream, bleaching, or going to a salon for a wax job. (Whatever you do, don't shave—that only makes things worse!) But the most important thing is to avoid obsessing and stressing over this. I mean, who you are and what you're worth as a person have no relation to how much peach fuzz you have on your arms.

Fiona

Bets <<I've learned that shaved arms, plucked eyebrows, almost everything except shaved legs really freaks out most guys.>>

Bets <<You're probably fine. It's just that models are waxed head to toe, so we think beautiful girls have no hair. Hair is beautiful and natural.>>

Tucker Says:

I'm a guy and all, but I have body image problems, too. In fact (and this is a nasty little secret), all guys do. All guys. I mean, there's a lot to be said for a hot body. Quite a lot, as a matter of fact. But once you've said it, you've said it. Then what? I'm talking about brains. About confidence. About attitude. About straight-up coolness. Those are the things I'm looking for.

'cause I've got such a big mouth. —Madonna

I'm Flat!

Q. Dear Fiona,

I have a problem. My chest is so small, and everyone makes fun of me! My best friend wears a D bra, and she's the same age as me! I haven't even made it to an A yet! I'm short for my age, but I'm not sure if that has anything to do with it. Everyone says it makes me look even more like a little kid, being flat chested and all. HELP!

—Flat in NYC

A. Hey, Flat,

Everyone has something about their bodies they don't like. Unfortunately, there usually isn't too much we can do about that—without resorting to extreme measures like plastic surgery. Which I personally think is gross and totally unnecessary.

Now, I know it's hard—especially if other people comment on it—but you gotta try to get over your insecurity about your breasts. Being flat-chested is part of who you are, and that's special. No matter what anyone says. So don't compare yourself to others, and don't think of your flatness as a flaw. Think of it as just another one of your characteristics.

And who knows if it's a permanent trait—you may still be developing—so there's a chance you could fill out. It is a genetic thing, though, so if your mom and your sisters aren't busty, chances are you won't be stacked, either. But that's okay. Breasts do not make the woman.

To me the point is to be strong but to still be a woman . . . I'm not

Still not convinced? Think about this: There are tons of big-breasted women out there who dream of being flatter.

Hang in there,

Fiona

Michelle <<Okay!!! Being flat ain't all that bad! I have a large chest, and it's not fun. . . . People assume I sleep around or something, but I have been with the same guy for five months.>>

Sassy <<Think how cool it is that you can wear halter tops without a bra. Sexy!>>

I hate my big boobs!

Q. Hey, Fiona,

My problem is that I have a really big chest (I mean really big—I'm in eighth grade and I'm already a D, even though I'm like a size 4 in clothes). I know that doesn't sound like a big deal—but it's making my life a total nightmare! I get teased all the time at school, by girls and guys. My mom says they're just jealous, but I don't know. I mean, people I barely know say I'm a slut, sometimes even to my face, and some girls won't talk to me because they think I'm trying to steal their boyfriends or something. But I'm not!

Plus the guys at school stare at my breasts—even my closest guy friends. And they bang into me a lot in the halls and stuff. I used to think I was just a klutz, but I've started to notice that it's only guys I stumble into.

What am I supposed to do? It's not like I can get rid of them. And will guys ever like me for anything more than the two ugly lumps of fat I happen to have attached to my body? I feel like they're the only things people notice about me anymore.

–Desperate

A. Hey, Desperate,

Okay, first of all, breasts come in all different sizes. Big, little, pointy, round, perky, saggy—I could go on and on. And that's completely normal. Also, some girls—like you—develop faster than others, and that's totally normal, too. So, I know it's hard, but try not to be so self-conscious about your breasts. There's nothing wrong with them, and more important, there's nothing wrong with you. Besides, they're going to be with you for a long time, so you might as well make peace with them now. The sooner you learn to accept (and love) them, the happier you'll be in the long run.

As for all those rumors, well, that's a little tougher. Having a large chest does not make you a slut, and it's beyond wrong for people to make such assumptions about you. But you know what? Unless you personally confront everyone whispering about you or sport a T-shirt with *I'm Stacked, but I Ain't a Hoochie* written on it (which I don't recommend), there's not really a whole lot you can do. You and the people who know and care about you know the truth, and that's what matters. Sooner or later, those gossips will either find a real scandal to talk about or finally mature a little. So you just need to keep on keepin' on.

Now for the big issue: the harassment. No one, I repeat, no one has the right to say offensive things or touch you without your permission—that includes both your male friends and those random feel coppers in the hallways. Forget that boys-will-be-boys excuse—it's sexual harassment and sexual assault. It creates a hostile learning environment, and that's a violation under Title IX of the Education Amendments of 1972. That means it's illegal, and your school (if it's federally funded) is legally bound to protect you. Many schools—both private and public—now have sexual harassment policies to help protect female students from this type of behavior (although admittedly, some are better at enforcing them than others). I know, no one likes to narc on their classmates, but this is one situation where you need to get authority figures involved. Because chances are, it won't stop or just go away on its own. Plus I bet you're not the only one getting harassed. So talk to a school counselor, your principal, or a teacher you trust about the situation. Now.

What can you personally do to help stop it? Don't laugh it

off or make a joke of it (something many girls do to hide their discomfort). Be firm. Make it very clear to your male classmates that they are not allowed to touch or grab you like that. You may also want to walk with your other female friends—that safety-in-numbers thing is true.

Stand up for yourself. Be strong.

Fiona

Courtney <<Maybe you should tell your best guy friend how much it sucks for you, and he can be on jerk patrol. >>

SmashMouth <<I had the same problem, and then my mom took me to this really good bra store and they fitted me (so embarrassing—but worth it!). Anyway, I got these great bras, and they made everything so much better. No more uniboob, but no swaying in the wind, either.>>.

NikiCool <<Breasts are part of what makes you a woman. You should be proud of them, not ashamed. My mother and sister have huge chests, and I have hardly anything. They are so womanly, and I feel like a little kid in comparison, but I can accept that. Learn to love your body, it is yours forever.>>.

It is never any good to oneself. —Oscar Wilde

Sleeps too much
Tissues
Gets sick a lot
BEER
Drinks to excess
No, I don't wanna meet this week.
555-1234
Blows off friends
Loses or gains a lot of weight
Geometry
F
Science
1.
2.
3.
4.
5
D
Grades drop

your head

Life can seriously suck sometimes. Like Fiona Apple once said, the world can be a piece of doody. (Only she didn't exactly say doody. . . .) You can't be happy every day.

And that's okay. If you were happy every day, you'd probably be suppressing the bad stuff.

Remember, no matter what you're going through—bad grades, bitchy friends, boredom—it will get better. You may even learn something from it. In my experience, the people who deal with the most adversity in their lives usually come out the strongest because of it.

But it's important to get an outside perspective on some things, so when you're feeling down, don't keep it quiet. Talk to your friends, your family, a teacher, or even a counselor—someone who will tell you what's doody and what's not.

Fiona

no one believes I'm depressed

Q. Dear Tucker,

I'm depressed. I mean, not just upset. I think I'm seriously depressed and have been for a long time. I keep hearing about depression and I'm always like, "That's me!" I always hear about all these things you can do to treat it, but no one in my family believes me. They know I'm bummed out and all, but my mother's always saying it's a phase or I'll get over it or something. Why won't she understand? What if it's more serious than that? Help!

–Blue Girl

A. Dear B.G.,

Yes, depression is real. Yes, it's serious. Yes, it's different from just being a little blue. Yes, there are things you can do about it. And no, not everyone understands. In fact, not everyone wants to. And unfortunately, sometimes the people you need the most are the people who just don't get it. It sucks to feel like you're not getting the support you want from your family. But it's a waste of your time and energy to worry about that right now. What you need to worry about is getting better. I mean, if you had a broken leg and no one believed you, you'd deal with the broken leg first, then deal with convincing everyone that you had one. Right? Reach out, and I mean reach out beyond your family. People at school—teachers, counselors, peer counselors, people like that—can help. And there are plenty of teen support groups (in your town, on-line, and otherwise) that can get you in touch with people who will believe you and who can help you get better. What's more, they'll even help you figure out how to get your family on your side. Don't wait for your parents to do something. Take your mind into your own hands and help yourself.

Tucker

Depression

Many of the letters Fiona and I get say something like, "I've got so much homework, I'm so depressed," but maybe we shouldn't toss the term around so carelessly. There's a big difference between being bummed out and being depressed. Depression is a serious condition, one that is important to identify and treat. Here are some symptoms to watch out for:

1. *Feeling very sad, tired, bored, pessimistic, hopeless, worthless, or helpless for an extended period (more than two weeks)*
2. *Getting more colds than you're used to*
3. *Having a hard time concentrating, or making decisions, or remembering things*
4. *Not being interested in things you normally really like*
5. *Blowing off friends and family all the time*
6. *Letting your grades drop big-time*
7. *Losing or gaining a lot of weight*
8. *Sleeping all the time or not being able to sleep at all*
9. *Drinking heavily or taking lots of drugs*
10. *Being overly harsh on people or violent*
11. *Getting physical sexually when you don't really want to*
12. *Being obsessed with dying and suicide*

If you're experiencing at least two of these symptoms, you need to seek professional help. Therapy is the best. You get to talk about yourself for a solid hour, and they have to listen. Not even your best friend will do that on demand!

So the next time you say, "I'm depressed," think about it. Are you really? Then help yourself and get help.

is patience. —Gautama Buddha

dropping grades

Q. Hey, Tucker,

Like three years ago I was supersmart. I liked school and got pretty much straight As. I wasn't some ass-kissin' prep, but I was smart. Now I'm in ninth grade and I can't do anything right—my grades are slipping down to C-minuses, and I'll just walk into the classroom sometimes and not understand a word the teacher says. I need help.

–C-minus Average

A. Hey, C-minus,

School gets harder as you go on. There's much more expected of you in ninth grade than there was in sixth. That's part of the deal—grow up, get harder homework. No way around it. Still, if you used to be such a great student, there might be something else going on. Maybe something in your life outside of school is stressing you out. Maybe your high school is more competitive than you ever expected. Maybe you're not getting enough sleep.

Not only does school get harder as you go along, but you become more responsible for identifying and solving your own

What do we live for if it is not to make life

problems. Most people in this situation would say, "Well, if I'm not doing so hot in school, then that means school sucks." You're wise enough to recognize that the problem is you. Luckily you caught it early. You have four more years to get it right.

Pick a teacher or school administrator you like and respect and give them the same note you wrote to me. Chances are, they'll have an answer for you—private tutoring, or a motivation class, or homework help. Don't let this go on too much longer without help, though. High school isn't all about schoolwork. Just think how much more fun you can have when you're not stressed about your grades anymore!

Good luck,

Tucker

PetR <<I had an older kid tutor me and teach me how to take notes. My grades have gone way up and I even like some of my classes more.>>

Cam <<You can be smart and still do badly. Good grades are all about studying no matter how smart or dumb you are. It does suck.>>

Belle <<If you get to pick electives try to pick things that interest you. Then it's easier to pay attention.>>

I can't take the pressure

Q. Dear Fiona,

I feel like I'm going to explode any second now!

My parents are putting way too much pressure on me about school. I'm a junior in advanced placement classes and I get mostly As and an occasional B. I have the best grades out of any of my friends and nearly everyone in my grade. But that's still not good enough for my parents. They want me to get straight As. They say that if I don't, I won't get into a good college.

It's bad enough that they're constantly on my back, lecturing me about applying myself, but they've also been letting me spend less and less time with my friends. They say I need to concentrate on what's really important and "give it 120 percent."

Help!

–Stressed

A. Hey, Stressed,

That totally sucks, you poor thing. Your parents should be supporting you!

You've got to talk to them—now—before they harass you a second longer.

I'm not saying you should disrespect your parents or anything. I'm sure they want what's best for you. But in this case, it sounds like they're in the wrong. They're getting too wrapped up with your report card—and they're forgetting about you.

Sure, good grades are important. But they're not everything. Your parents shouldn't make you feel like they are. And they shouldn't deprive you of your hang-out time, either. You need a break from studying, or you'll crack up for sure.

No one can take that much pressure. It's unhealthy and unnecessary, and it's probably not helping you get better grades. So set up a time to talk to them and tell them to lighten up on the pressure. Assure them that you can still get As and spend quality time with your friends. Work out a compromise, and then stick to it!

And don't forget to take a deep breath and exhale!

Fiona

buggin <<Your parents need to lay off and let you be your own person. It sounds like you put enough pressure on yourself. >>

2wack <<Your parents should be telling you how great you are.>>

I want to commit suicide

Q. Dear Fiona,

Hey, my name is Matt. I suffer from depression, and I'm constantly thinking about suicide and how I'm going to end it all. I need help.

But I don't want to tell my parents because I would seem like a failure—and I don't really want their help. Please just tell me what I can do to stop wanting to kill myself.

—Matt

A. Dear Matt,

First off: Please do not kill yourself. I don't know what you're going through right now—but whatever it is, it is definitely not worth ending your life over.

No matter how major your problems seem at the moment, they're never so huge that you can't find a way through them. It's never as bad as you think, and there's always someone you can talk to, who will help you. It's senseless to do something so rash, and so permanent, as kill yourself.

And another thing: Killing yourself doesn't only affect you. Think of the people in your life who love you and would be devastated if you weren't alive. Ending your life isn't simple—you'll be hurting everyone who cares about you. (And be honest with yourself—they do care.)

Normally I'd tell you to talk to your parents. But if you absolutely don't want to discuss it with them, then you should talk to a friend, teacher, counselor, doctor, or some other adult you trust. Or if you don't feel comfortable talking to someone you know, get free, anonymous help from a suicide prevention organization or hot line.

There's no problem that's that bad, I swear. If you hang in there, you'll see. And please get yourself some help. You already said you wanted it—so reach out and get it. Now.

Peace,

Fiona

DD <<Don't do it! This is the only life you'll ever have.>>

Gret <<It's not cool to be dead.>>

Mile2 <<My brother killed himself and it ruined our family. It will ruin yours too. It's good you know you want to do it and you want to stop thinking about it. Get help now.>>

For suicide help lines, see p. 170.

club. —Wendy O'Connor, Kurt Cobain's mother

I'm depressed, should I tell him?

Q. Hey, Tucker,

I've been diagnosed with depression. I can deal with it okay, but should I tell my boyfriend? Last time I saw him, I was seriously considering breaking up with him just because I didn't want him to see me so messed up. I don't want him worrying about me too much, especially since I think I have a handle on what's wrong. But part of me thinks he has a right to know. Should I tell him or just say everything's all right?

–Chica

A. Chica,

Here's my rule about disclosing superpersonal information like that: Only tell people if you think it will help you. No one has a "right" to know.

See, by far the most important thing for you right now is to concentrate on yourself. Being diagnosed with depression is major, and you need to do whatever it takes to deal with that situation first. That means surrounding yourself with lots of people who will help you out and give you support—your family and old friends, rather than people who take energy away from you. Maintaining a relationship can be very draining, especially a new relationship. Right now you need people to lift you up, not drag you down.

So I think you have a bigger decision on your hands. That is, do you want to stay with this guy through this, or do you want to take a break and concentrate on yourself for a while? If you think he's not the kind of guy you'd feel comfortable telling, I'm not so sure he'd be all that great to have around. But if you think he's the kind of guy who'd give you help and support, then spill your guts.

Good luck,

Tucker

sullengirl <<I can relate to you. I've also been diagnosed with depression. I don't tell anyone that I don't feel will be understanding and supportive.>>

tellit <<I would tell him. You will feel relieved no matter how he reacts. If he cares about you he will be okay with it and just want you to get better.>>

Myk <<Depression is pretty common. For all you know he's on Prozac.>>

Friendship Rules!

your friends

Best friends rule! But having friends isn't all joy. It takes real work to maintain those friendships. Respect, understanding, flexibility, forgiveness, kindness. I've been dissed more times than I'd like to remember by good friends—not because they were trying to hurt me, but because they took me for granted. And I'm sure I've dissed plenty of my friends for the same reasons.

Here's what I've learned. Friendships are relationships. It's funny how once you use the word *relationship*, all of a sudden you start thinking about the effort it takes. A relationship feels like a long-lasting, deep, important thing. Kind of like, oh, I don't know, a friendship!

Your friends will always be there for you. That is, if you treat 'em right.

Tucker

cover up

Q. Dear Fiona,

My friend keeps asking me to cover for her. She just got her driver's license, and so she always wants to go visit guys. She tells her mom that she's at my house and then tells me to lie if her mom calls. One day she almost got caught, and she told me that I couldn't leave to go see my great-grandmother and that if I did leave, it would be my fault that she got in trouble. We've been friends for a really long time, and I don't want this to cause us to stop being friends—but she's really beginning to make me mad.

–kermie

A. Dear kermie,

You have every right to be totally mad. What does your friend think—just 'cause she scored a driver's license, you should spend your time hangin' by the telephone in case her mom decides to randomly call and check up on her? Hello! You have a life, too—and I'm guessing there are other things you'd rather be doing with it than phone patrol. If I were you, I'd explain to her that while you consider her a great friend and would do whatever you could to help her (within reason), it's unfair and really selfish of her to ask you to cover for her like that all the time. And for her to pull a guilt trip on you is also seriously lame. It's not your fault if she gets busted for lying to her parents—it's hers!

But there's a much more important reason not to keep covering up for her. Say your friend was driving around and her car broke down, or worse, she got into an accident. Her mom already checked in with you, so you left the house. She probably wouldn't have anyone else to turn to. She could be stranded on the side of the road without anyone to help her for who knows how long. And you would be partly responsible! The reason why her parents want to know where she's going in the first place is to prevent that kind of thing from happening.

Tell it like it is,

Fiona

Carol <<Wake up! She's using you! Tell her to kiss it!>>

Melissa <<Next time she asks, tell her flat out no. If she gets mad, don't worry 'cause she's bound to get over it and if she doesn't, then she's not worth it at all.>>

when your face is dirty.—Sicilian proverb

my friend is obsessed with her boyfriend

Q. Hey, Tucker,

My best friend has a boyfriend, and I think that she spends way too much time with him. He takes her to school, sees her several times a day, spends every day after school with her till at least nine-thirty, and if they can't possibly be together, they're on the phone, even if they have nothing to say. I feel like I'm losing her to him and it feels like she's losing herself to him. Help!

–Losing

I have a healthy cynicism,

A. Dear Losing,

There's nothing more frustrating than feeling like a best friend has replaced you with a boyfriend. On the one hand, you're happy they're having a love life. On the other hand, you're left twiddling your thumbs. But at the same time you worry about your friend, not wanting her to get hurt or whatever.

First—don't judge their relationship. Even if you think they're spending too much time together, it's not really your place to speak up. Besides, they won't hear you, and they'll just get annoyed and hurt. Let them make their own mistakes.

Next—start spending your time doing other stuff besides waiting around for her. Call some other friends and hang with them. It's time to live your own life.

Go to it!

Tucker

Happy <<My friend is doing the same thing. But I told her how I felt, and now we hang out all the time.>>

Mindy <<She may say you're just jealous, but it does hurt you, so you need to tell her how you feel. . . . Then you two can work it out so she spends time with you, too. Maybe you can all go out together.>>

but not anger. —Sheryl Crow

my friend owes me $$

Q. Tucker

My best friend is constantly bugging me for money. When we go to the mall, she'll want me to buy her something, and if I don't give her money, she says she'll do something really embarrassing in front of a bunch of people. I tell her no, but she keeps on asking and she gets on my nerves so I just give it to her. She says she'll pay me back, but she never has any money and when she does, she won't pay me back! She owes me like $45—I know it may not sound like a lot, but when you're 14 and work really hard baby-sitting, it is. What should I do?

—money girl

A. Hello, money girl. Anyone home?

Never again will you give this girl a cent. Period. Understand?

No one who is supposed to be your friend would manipulate you into giving her cash over and over again, even threatening to cause a scene if you refuse. That is truly uncool.

Under normal circumstances, I might give you some ideas of exactly what to say to her to get her to back off, but these aren't normal circumstances. This chick is straight up using you. So you need to straight up tell her to stick it next time she asks for some dough.

Afraid of losing a friend? Don't be. She doesn't seem like much of a friend, and if she really is, then she'll get it and change her ways. The way she's acting she's going to run out of friends fast. Stop giving her money, ask her to pay you back, and

Money doesn't make you happy. I now have $50 million but I was tell her how much it bothers you. If she's worth keeping as a friend, she'll pay up.

Out,

Tucker

Katie <<Your friend doesn't have the cash to pay you back? You may have some chores that need doing. . . .>>

Copa Cabana <<Tell her that she sucks and she should get a stinking job!!!>>

just as happy when I had $48 million. —Arnold Schwarzenegger

help! I just kissed my best friend's boyfriend!

Q. Dear Fiona,

I'm in serious trouble here. See, my best friend has the coolest, cutest boyfriend in the world. We've always been good friends (I even got them together), but I've always kind of had a secret crush on him. Here's the problem: Last night he drove me home from a party, and as I leaned over to hug him good-bye, we ended up kissing. It was just one kiss, and no one else knows about it. I'm totally freaking out over this, though. What should I do? Say nothing or tell my friend about it? I think she'd totally hate my guts if she knew the truth. Help!

–S. M.

A. Hey, S. M.,

If there's any chance that your friend is going to find out, it had better be from you. If she gets the news of your illicit smooch from anyone else—her boyfriend, her sister, the school gossip, whoever—you're really going to be in deep, deep trouble. So you have to decide what you're going to do. As I see it, there are two options. You could talk to her guy and make a pact to never, ever tell anyone. But not only is that deceiving your friend, it's also taking the risk that you'll get busted if one of you slips and tells even one other person. (You know how hard it is to keep a secret, right?) So personally, I think the best plan of action is to tell your friend what happened. Right away. And promise her that it was just a one-time thing and that you'll keep your

Advice is what we ask for when we already know

hands—and lips—off her man for all eternity. She may be mad (at both of you) at first, but she should get over it. It was just one kiss. And you're never, ever, ever going to let it happen again, right?

It will turn out okay.

Fiona

Jam <<I think that you should talk to her boyfriend and see how he feels about the kiss. It may have meant more than you think.>>

10 Reasons Not to Dis Your Girls for a Guy

10. *They can talk on-line, watch TV, and do their homework with you all at the same time without getting distracted.*
9. *They never get sick of your favorite movie.*
8. *They let you borrow their clothes.*
7. *They'll dance with you—anywhere.*
6. *They don't blame every one of your bad moods on PMS.*
5. *They've seen you at your dorkiest and didn't run screaming.*
4. *They call you on it when you're out of line.*
3. *You aren't embarrassed when they come over and talk to your parents.*
2. *You aren't embarrassed when they see you cry.*
1. *Unless you do something absolutely unforgivable, they'll never break up with you.*

the answer but wish we didn't. —Erica Jong

my friend is suicidal

Q. Hey, Tucker,

This guy friend of mine has gone totally suicidal. He cuts himself, drinks tons of beer, won't talk to anyone. When he finally does talk to someone, he won't look them in the face. His mom is no help with his problems because she's a real witch and only tells him how bad he is. I really want to help this guy because he has tons of potential but has such low self-esteem. What is the best thing I can do for him without letting him get too attached to me since he can be clingy with girls?

Thanks.

—Forever Grateful!

A. Hey, Forever,

That sucks. But here's the deal. This guy is obviously way out there with problems and stuff. He's got some serious issues. The best thing you can do for him is exactly what you're doing already—making it clear you're there if he needs you.

The bottom line is, you aren't going to save this guy. You may be the most awesome, intelligent, helpful, kind, supportive friend in the world, but his problems are way too huge for you to solve on your own. I know how difficult it is to watch someone self-destruct like that, especially someone you love. But there's only so much you can do.

Talk to other people who might be able to help him—his father, a teacher, or maybe a school counselor (believe it or not, those people can be really useful sometimes). Knowing that people care about him will help him.

Don't lead me; I may not follow. Don't walk behind me;

But don't forget to take care of yourself, too.
Peace,

Tucker

Izzy <<Talk to him about why he's so depressed, give him advice, or give him phone numbers to call about depression—tell him good things about him!>>

Rianne <<I read somewhere that you should always take suicide threats seriously. Not everyone who threatens actually does it, but everyone who does it has threatened at some point. So get help!>>

For depression and suicide help lines, see p. 170.

my friend's turning into a druggie

Q. Help, Tucker!

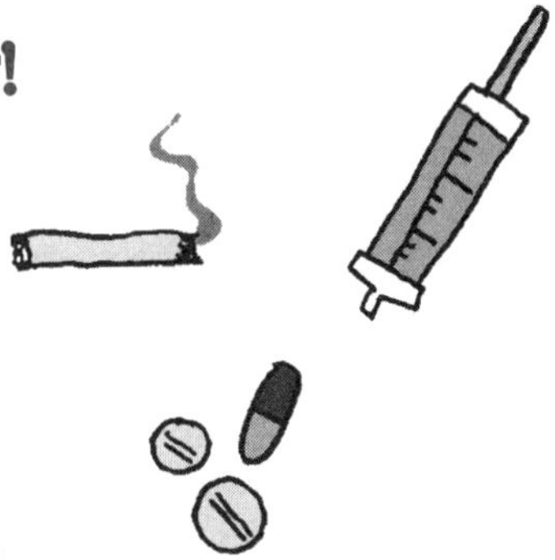

My friend started dating this guy a few months ago, and he's completely messed her up. He was always known as a big pothead at school, and now that she's dating him, she's doing lots of drugs, too. Every time she hangs out with her old friends (like me), all she talks about are her acid trips or mushrooms or pot. I don't think she's done anything dangerous (yet), but I'm worried that she will soon. I want to help her, but every time I say something, she tells me I'm being stupid. I just want my friend back!

—All Worried

A. Okay, All Worried,

Ugh. It sucks when your friends don't act like themselves. It's so annoying when a friend starts acting like her boyfriend all the time—dressing like him, listening to his music, or doing his drugs.

But the sad part is, there's not a lot you can do. People need to make their own mistakes. You've told her that you're concerned and that you want her to be happy and healthy (right?), but she's still not listening. You could go one step further and do a little research to give her more facts so she'll make better

I guess happiness is not a state you

decisions, but there may come a point where you need to just throw up your hands, say, "Not my problem!" and let her go. Hopefully she'll find her way back to reality soon.

Good luck,

Tucker

P.S. She has done dangerous stuff. In 1999 someone drowned and died at a beach on Long Island while he was on mushrooms. Thousands of people tripping on acid end up in emergency rooms every year. And driving high is just as dangerous and serious as driving drunk.

Heidi <<She's ruining her own life, and the only thing you can do is talk to her–keep trying. Sit her down when you two are alone and make her listen.>>

For drug abuse help lines, see p. 170.

Tucker says:

A friend of mine is in a coma right now, lying in a hospital with tubes sticking out all over. They drilled a hole in his head to drain excess fluid. He's got a 25 percent chance of recovering and a 75 percent chance of being a vegetable for the rest of his life. He wasn't a drug addict or anything. He's an amazing guy who got into the wrong batch of crank.

No matter what you think, you have no idea what you're putting into your body when you take drugs. Some freak who probably didn't even pass chemistry is off in a warehouse somewhere mixing up X or cutting coke or whatever, making the recipes up as he goes along. And he's probably messed up on drugs while he's doing it.

Talk about scary.

want to be in all the time. —John Belushi

my friend can't say no to boys

Q. Dear Fiona,

Recently my friend and I got into an argument about how she just lets guys do whatever they want to her. I mean it—if they want her body, they have it, no questions asked.

She always gets hurt when this happens. Then she comes crying to me, and I always get caught in the middle. When I try to tell her that she shouldn't just give herself up, she gets all huffy and says that I don't know anything because I'm not "experienced" in that field. She asks me for help, and then she blows me off when she doesn't like what she hears.

I don't know how to get it through this girl's thick head that she's a hoochie (everyone calls her that) and needs to stop what she's doing before she gets some sort of disease! I've tried to help her clean up her act, but every time I'm even close to doing it, she goes fooling around again.

Can you please help me out?!

–Concerned

A. Dear Concerned,

Sometimes people ask for advice when they don't really want it. This is definitely the deal with your friend. When she's feeling used and abused, she runs to you for consolation. She doesn't want to hear that she's been a "hoochie"—so she shoots you down, saying that you're sexually inexperienced and couldn't possibly understand what she's going through.

It is possible that blondes

The truth is, you're right, she's wrong, and you said what you said because you were trying to be a good friend. So don't feel bad. Obviously you're worried about your friend's mental and physical health—and those are real concerns, considering how much she fools around.

But here's the bottom line: This is her problem, not yours. You can talk all you want, but she may not listen. Try not to get mad the next time she lashes out at you, though. Understand that she's hurting, and try to be there for her as best you can.

Peace,

Fiona

QT Pie <<She's just looking for someone to tell her that everything's all right and to ease her conscience.>>

Hello Kitty <<Maybe she's got a self-esteem problem. Maybe she lets guys do stuff to her because it makes her feel important. You have to tell her she's important in other ways.>>

Fiona says:

No matter what your friends' little quirks or issues are—no matter who's selfish, who's a hoochie, or whatever, you have to forget the petty differences and remember that when it comes to friendship, what really matters is how you treat each other.

also prefer gentlemen. —Mamie Van Doren

my best friend is crushing on my guy!

Q. Dear Fiona,

Okay. My friend and I were having a sleep over, and I asked her, out of any person in the whole world, who she wanted to go out with. Guess who she said! My boyfriend!

At first I tried to be understanding and put myself in her position, but now it makes me uncomfortable to leave them alone. Maybe I don't trust him, but I can't believe she'd tell me that. It makes being around her very difficult. She's my best friend, and we've been friends forever.

I don't know what to do—break up with him and let

her have him or tell her, "Tough luck—find your own man!"

Help!!!
–Me

A. Dear Me,

Yikes! Yeah, your friend definitely dropped a big, fat bomb on you. Here's how to defuse it:

Resist the urge to go ballistic on her. After all, you are best friends. But let her know that it's totally uncool for her to lust after your boyfriend. I mean, there are tons of guys out there—but only one you. Couldn't she find someone else to crush on? Let her know that you feel betrayed.

As for how to deal with your boyfriend, there's nothing to do. Why break up with him? He obviously likes you—that's why he's with you. So don't let your friend's revelation make you feel insecure about that.

Hang in there,

Fiona

Eve <<You should be flattered. It just means she thinks your boyfriend's cool. If she's a good friend, she won't try to steal him from you.>>

Diglt<<Don't be mad unless she talks about how much she likes him all the time. And definitely don't even mention it to him. That will only cause tension beween all three of you.>>

would be no need for argument.—Chuang Tzu, Chinese philosopher

my friend betrayed me

Q. Dear Fiona,

One of my best friends has betrayed me. I told her a really personal secret, and I know she told! I overheard her talking to a whole bunch of people about me—and afterward she wouldn't even look at me! I felt like crying.

This secret was big, and she was the only one I trusted with it. Now I want to tell everyone her secret—how she did the exact same thing! I'm so depressed! She won't even talk to me—not even to say sorry.

—so very sad

A. Dear S.U.S.,

Why can't people can't keep their mouths shut—especially people you're supposed to trust? The way I see it, you've got two issues here: how to deal with the trauma of having your secret spilled, and how to deal with your so-called friend.

In terms of the secret—whatever it is—there's not much you can do except let it blow over. And although it might not seem likely, it will blow over. Eventually. So try not to worry about it too much.

But you have to take a more active approach in dealing with your friend. She definitely deserves a piece of your mind—and you deserve some answers. So make her talk to you. I don't know what could've made her turn on you, but there's definitely no excuse for it.

Even if she apologizes, I'd think long and hard before trusting her with something major again. And if she doesn't apologize? Ditch her. But don't blab her secret because that will just keep the whole drama on everyone's minds. Which won't help you.

Hang in there,

Fiona

life-or-death secret

Q. Dear Tucker,

I have a really close friend who wants me to keep a secret. This is something that really should be made known because it could be a matter of life or death. But I don't want to lose my friend's trust. What should I do?

—confused friend

A. Dear confused,

This is a tough one. The thing about secrets is, well, it's not easy to sit with them. Most of the time you pretty much know what the consequences would be if you spoke up. If it was a little piece of gossip like "Jenny likes Jeff" and you told, Jenny would be mad, but everyone would get over it. But when the secret is about something that could potentially really hurt someone, it's more complex. If you tell, your friend might be mad at you. But if you don't tell, your friend might be in danger.

Talk to your friend. Say something like, "You've put me in a really messed-up situation. I want to do what's best for you. I want to help. Help me decide what to do." Maybe she'll agree to let you tell or even talk to someone

When in doubt,

herself. If this doesn't work, you've got to wrestle with your conscience and make a choice yourself. When I have to make a tough decision, I always sleep on it, and the first answer that comes to my head when I wake up is the one I go with.

Good luck,

Tucker

Julia <<Whatever you do, you should respect her wishes. She trusts you!>>

Tracy <<When someone tells you these things and asks you not to tell anyone, it's just like a cry for help! Tell an adult, and help your friend!>>

Fiona says:

There's a huge difference between spilling a secret when you absolutely have to and talking trash. Sometimes you have to speak up to help someone or to set a bad situation straight. In situations like those, it's the right thing to do. Even if it might piss people off at first.

But if you're blabbing for selfish reasons—to make yourself feel superior to others, to gain popularity, to hurt someone, or just for the fun of keeping the rumor mill spinning—be assured, it will come back to you. And over time, folks will lose respect for you because of it.

The strongest, coolest people I know don't gossip. They've got too much going on in their own lives to mouth off about other people. And when others try to spread dirt about them, they're unfazed. Because even the best piece of gossip eventually just blows over.

tell the truth. —Mark Twain

I have no friends anymore

Q. Hey, Tucker!

I have this problem. I don't want to go back to school because last year I lost all my very good friends over a stupid fight that I started (and I wish I hadn't). Now almost everyone is mad at me, and I practically have no friends! What should I do?

—Anonymous

A. Hey, Anon!

Time to suck it up and start apologizing.

I don't know what the fight was about, but most of the time a good old apology (and a good amount of time, like a summer's worth) will do the trick. But here's the catch: You have to mean it.

You've told me that you're responsible for what happened, so I hope you're willing to say the same to them. And if I were you, I'd do it as soon as possible.

There is a possibility they won't forgive you, which means you'll have to find some new friends. Facing the people you pissed off sounds scary, but the alternative—hiding at home all year—sounds even worse.

Be brave,

Tucker

Btrue <<Props to you for admitting you were in the wrong. Once you've apologized, though, don't let them throw it back in your face all the time—that's not cool.>>

Callie <<You have to patch it all up or you'll regret it. I lost my best friend this way, and when I tried to get her back, it was too late. I regret it every day. React fast! Good luck!>>

miss popularity

Q. Hey, Fiona,

My so-called best friend ignores me and doesn't tell me anything anymore. She's always hanging around with more popular people. When we ride the bus together, she acts like we've been nonstop best friends, but as soon as she enters school, she's a totally different person. I think she's embarrassed to be around me. What's going on?

–Chelsi

A. Dear Chelsi,

we talk on the bus
but she ignores me in school.

It sounds like your friend is trying to work her way into the cool clique and thinks that she has to dis you in order to do that. But she can't treat you one way when you two are alone and another way when you're in school. That's unfair. So sit her down and tell her how you feel, and if she doesn't change, give her the same treatment she's giving you.

Most likely, she'll come around and realize that your friendship is worth more to her than being part of the in crowd. Let's face it—as tempting as the concept of popularity may be, the reality isn't always that great.

One last thing: If Miss Popularity doesn't get it together soon, go out and make some new friends. It sounds to me like you're a pretty deep and loyal gal, and most people—at least the nonsuperficial types—will value that.

Good luck,

Fiona

Pattie <<The popular kids at my school walk around like they have corn chips up their @$$. Find new friends who don't care about hanging out with snobs.>>

Jon <<She's not your friend if she thinks she's too good for your friendship. So find some new friends. When she's no longer "Miss Thang," she'll come crawling back asking you to forgive her.>>

Fiona says:

Here's my theory about being in a cool clique. It makes you feel powerful, but in actuality you're weak, relying on others to define who you are. When you're in a clique, you get your self-esteem from who you hang with but you're excluding others and keeping them down. Then when school's over and you don't have that false sense of strength anymore, there's not a whole lot left of you.

as long as it isn't true. —Truman Capote

three's a crowd

Q. Dear Fiona,

I have two best friends, and they make me feel totally left out. One minute they act so great and I love them, but the next they'll start talking about "inside stuff," as they put it, and they won't stop giggling about it. It makes me feel like such a loser. What should I do?

—Kaiherine

A. Hey, Kaiherine,

Ouch. Okay, here's what you do. The next time your friends are whispering about their "inside stuff," tell them how hurt and left out you feel. Don't completely freak out on them or anything—

just let them know that their behavior is bumming you out. If they really care, they'll listen to what you have to say and try to change their ways.

If not, then it may be time to start finding some new friends because good friends should only make life better, not more traumatic. So join a club or sports team or even just ask that really cool girl who sits next to you in English if she wants to catch a movie this weekend. By widening your circle of friends, you'll meet someone—or two or three or four someones—who's into the same stuff as you are and who will treat you right.

Hang in there.

Fiona

Shooby ***<<Be your own best friend. That's what I do. That doesn't necessarily make you a loser, just someone who prefers to be alone, and that's pretty cool.>>***

Caroline ***<<Find new friends. It sounds like they suck.>>***

Reg ***<<If you start ignoring them and doing your own thing, they'll get sick of each other and start calling you. Maybe you won't even miss them, and you'll make some better friends.>>***

like you intend it. —Diane Arbus

I'm a loner

Q. Dear Fiona,

I'm a total loner. I don't belong to any group of friends. I just hang out with whoever. I don't have a best friend or anything. The girl I hang out with a lot isn't even that close to me. I try to be friends with people. But I just don't seem to fit in.

–Alone

A. Hey, Alone,

Wow. I'm sorry to hear you're so lonely. I totally feel for you.

But even though you feel pretty hopeless right now, you have to believe me—there are things you can do to make friends. You've probably heard them all before, but I swear they really work. Here goes . . .

Before you can make friends, you have to meet people, right? No one's just going to come over to your house, ring your doorbell, and ask you to be their buddy. So you have to get out there. Join a club, a sports team, a yoga class, whatever. You're guaranteed to meet some cool people—you just have to be open to getting to know them, and you have to allow them to get to know you, too.

And when you meet someone you think you could bond with, you have to work at it. Friendship doesn't come easy. It's all about communicating, listening, and compromise. Chances are, you're not going to find a perfect friend, but that's not what matters—the important thing is to find someone who'll be there for you.

Good luck,

Fiona

JackieJ <<Yeah, I feel for you. I think a lot of teenagers feel this way. You just have to tell yourself that they are no different from you.>>

Tucker says:

At some point you may be the one giving advice. Remember, every situation is unique, and every situation is complex. Even a situation that seems common or simple isn't common or simple at all to the person who's dealing with it. That's why the number one rule for giving advice is: LISTEN. Don't attempt to solve the problem in twenty seconds flat. Instead shut up, turn off your judgment-o-meter, and pay attention to what the person is saying. Even if you think you've heard it before.

And remember this, too: It's okay if you don't have the answer. Nine times out of ten, people asking for advice already know what to do—they just need to talk it through to be sure. And ten times out of ten, the confidence they gain from knowing that you're truly listening and that you truly care will help them more than you can imagine.

You're here for mine. —Johnny Rotten of the Sex Pistols

LOVE

your crushes

Anyone who never wants to go out with me in a zillion years, do this: Come up to me and say, "I really, really like you. A lot. Like, I really, really like you." This is the fastest way to send any guy running. When someone tells you something like that, it's usually followed by a stare, like you're supposed to say the same thing right back. It's like an insta-pressure bomb. And it can be a huge shock coming from someone who hardly knows you at all.

If you have a crush on someone, it's best to say it without really saying it—know what I mean? Show them you're into them by getting to know them. And by giving them a chance to get to know you. If it turns out you get along and you want to take it to the next level, you'll let both know it soon enough.

Tucker

I'm crushing on the new guy

Q. Hey, Tucker!

There's this new guy at school. He is so good-looking, he's totally my type, and he seems to like me, too. He's in one of my classes, so I'm just starting to get to know him. Sometimes he acts like he's way into me, and we totally flirt. But then there are other times (like when he's around his new guy friends) when he acts like I'm the last person he ever wants to see. I want to get together with him, but I can't tell what he thinks of me.

----Spaced----

A. Hey, ----Spaced----,

Slow down! This guy is new and, well, he's a guy. He's got to find guy friends and girl friends before he goes looking for a girlfriend. He probably wouldn't flirt with you if he didn't think you were cute. But that doesn't mean he wants to be with you. He doesn't even know you yet. And you don't know him, either.

Remember that he has a lot to deal with right now. He's trying to make new friends, look cool, get decent grades, flirt with the girls, pick up new extracurriculars, and probably tons more. Try to get to know him better first—he may not be your type at all! But if you get along and the flirtation is still happening, there's a chance it could turn into something.

For now, there's nothing you can do but wait.

Tucker

Buffy <<Hey if you don't grab him, someone else will!>>

NEW
BOY

is he over her yet?

Q. Okay, Tucker,

How long does it take for a guy to get over a girl? I know that girls take a long time, but are guys just as slow? Because this guy just got dumped, and I want to know when to start flirting with him. Oh yeah, it wasn't a very serious relationship.

–Waiting

A. Dear Waiting,

Sorry, there's no real answer to your question.

See, every situation is different, and every guy is different. A guy who's really in love may never completely get over the girl he's lost—even though he might move on, he'll still have a crush on her. A guy who's a real player or just into casual relationships may not even remember the girl's last name the week after they break up. In other words, you never really know.

But how you tell if it's okay to flirt with a guy? Flirt with him! You'll know within thirty seconds whether or not it's working—your gut will tell you, loudly.

Let him worry about whether or not he's ready.

Later,

Tucker

Cam <<If you're good friends with him and he's still talking about her a lot, then he probably isn't over her yet. I would wait at least a week or two, and if he starts looking like he's in better spirits, then start flirting!!>>

If you greatly desire something, have the

Psssf <<Just flirt a little. If he flirts back, that may be a good thing. But he could still have baggage. If so, he might be using you to make her jealous—watch out!>>

JJ <<If it wasn't serious then he's probably already looking for someone new. You may be too late!>>

guts to stake everything on obtaining it. —Brendan Francis

my best friend is crushing on me

Q. Dear Tucker,

I just recently found out that my best friend of all time, who just happens to be a guy, has a huge crush on me. He didn't tell me, a friend of his did, and now I'm sworn to secrecy, so he has no idea that I know. I love the boy dearly, but I just don't feel the same way he does. So where do I go from here? Do I let him know that I know? Or do I wait? How can I tell him how I feel and keep our friendship intact?!

Slurpy

A. Here's the deal, *Slurpy*:

Don't do anything. See, you have a piece of information that you're not really supposed to have—someone told you something that they weren't supposed to tell you in the first place.

If your friend has a crush on you, then it's up to him to do something about it, not you. In other words, it's his crush, not yours. Unless he brings it up, you shouldn't discuss it with him. (Besides, he might get over it faster than you can imagine!) You have no choice but to keep treating him the same way you always have . . . since he's such a great friend, you owe him that.

If you say something, you risk freaking him out and ruining your friendship with him—not to mention his friendship with his "friend" who told you the news in the first place.

There are things to confess that enrich the world,

Keep it quiet,

Tucker

Fashion Nugget <<Don't act weird around him, or he'll definitely know something's up. Wait for him to ask you out, then tell him how you feel.>>

a loser wants to hook up with me

Q. Tucker!

This pale-faced, sicko, clumsy, not-my-type jerk has a huge crush on me. He's not my type at all but I actually think he's kind of cute. Why does he like me? Why do I like him??

Help!
–Kitty

Reality leaves a lot

A. Kitty!

You've just discovered one of the most important rules of life—that there's absolutely no accounting for taste. There's no rhyme or reason to who you crush on. It happens on a totally different level, and none of it makes sense.

But is there really anything wrong with it? Nope. If we only crushed on the people who are "perfect," things would get really boring really fast. It's all about finding that special little tingle someplace unexpected.

And another thing: Lots of times your friends or whoever will tell you your crush is a total loser, or not crush-worthy, or all kinds of other things. You've got to ignore this and remember it's your crush, not theirs.

Do cancel the crush if he's mean or cruel. But if he's just a weirdo, go with it. Either you'll get over it, or you'll end up putting your finger on what it is that made you crush in the first place.

Happy angsting!

Tucker

Sugar ***<<What's wrong with being pale?!>>***

Susie ***<<I've been in love with a clumsy dude for three years! Don't sweat it! Because when he spills his popcorn in the movie theater and reaches over you to pick some of it up and goes back to his seat, he'll accidentally end up holding your hand!>>***

I'm falling for my friend

Q. Dear Fiona,

I can't get my best friend of almost ten years out of my mind! I think I may be falling for him. I've had dreams about him, I'm curious about the idea of us dating, and almost every single person on the planet believes we are dating.

We share the same everything! We finish each other's sentences, reminisce about days in early childhood together, and laugh at the same things, and I know I can ask him all of my stupid philosophical questions. I can tell him anything!

But thing is, he's all I've got friendwise. I don't think I could take it if he rejected me as a girlfriend or, even worse, as his best friend.

For now, I've decided to wait and see if these feelings will go away, but so far it's gotten worse and worse. I'm afraid I'll let something slip. Please help!

—A. C.

A. Dear A. C.,

Okay, the point is, unless you go for it, you'll never know. And that would be brutal.

If you two are really as close as you say, then even if you make a move and he's not into it, he'll get over it. Quickly. Take my word for it. The same thing happened to me a few years back—and even though things didn't work out romantically (and believe me, it was all for the best), it didn't hurt our friendship one bit. Sure, there was some initial weirdness between us, but now we joke about it. And we're better friends than ever.

Never let the fear of striking

So I say, don't just stand there—bust a move.

Good luck,

Fiona

Cagey <<I kissed my best friend and we never spoke again. I'd try and keep the friendship–sometimes that can even be better.>>

Patsy <<I think that you should tell him how you feel. I mean, he might like you, but he might just be hiding it. You never know until you try.>>

Trick <<Just go out and hold his hand and look into his eyes. It sounds like you know him well enough to know what he's thinking. You'll know if you can take it any further.>>

Tucker says:

Sometimes when you spend all your time with someone and you know each other inside and out, they start looking pretty hot. But think about it: You have a fight with your boyfriend and you break up. You have a fight with your friend and you make up.

your dating dilemmas

When you're in high school, hooking up with and dating someone can seem like the most important thing ever. But in the grand scheme of things, it's not everything. You've got a lot more important things to worry about. Like school. Like your friends. Like those guitar lessons you've been meaning to take.

And the thing is, the more you focus on those parts of your life, the more complete and interesting a person you'll be. And that's what makes you attractive to other people, anyway. So instead of looking for someone special, why not work on the things that make you special? People will notice you for that, not because of who you've hooked up with. And believe me, you will be found whether you want to be or not.

Fiona

I'm dreading my dinner date

Q. Dear Fiona,

It took me and this guy so long to finally do something together because I was so scared. Now we're going out to dinner! I've never been on a date, and I hate eating in front of guys I don't know very well. Should I eat differently?

—Eating Distress

A. Hey, E. D.,

Congratulations for scoring a date with your crush object. I'm sure you guys will have a total blast together . . . unless you're all uptight about something. Which is why you have to get over this eating issue. In our diet-obsessed culture, people have become ashamed of eating—even though it's a normal, necessary part of life. Not to mention a fun social activity.

You probably won't change your food attitude overnight. But you've got to order something. Here are some damage-control tips. Avoid: spaghetti (twisting and slurping those noodles can get pretty messy), shellfish and crustaceans (digging out clams and cracking lobster claws is dangerous business), and chopsticks (unless you're a master, you could wind up flinging food in your date's face). Whatever you do, don't order just a salad! It's totally cliché, your stomach will be rumbling the rest of the night, and you're pretty much guaranteed to get something green stuck between your teeth!

Try not to worry about what you order or how you look while you're eating—I guarantee he's not stressing over those things—and concentrate on getting to know your date better. The most important thing to remember: chill out and have fun!

Fiona

KIR <<My boyfriend loves to go out with me because he says I'm the only girl he knows who actually eats in front of her boyfriend!>>

Thomas <<Don't be scared, be yourself. He likes you for who you are, so don't try changing yourself because he might not like you anymore.>>

he won't pay for me

Q. Dear Fiona,

I've been dating my boyfriend for almost three months, and we go out all the time. I love this guy to death, but my problem is that he never pays for me. He invites me to go to the movies or dinner or lunch—and he doesn't pay! The only time he paid was the first night he asked me to the movies, and since then he hasn't done it.

Homecoming is this weekend, and I have no money for anything!!! What should I do?

–Katie

A. Hey, Katie,

Okay, if your boyfriend sticks you with paying for everything (for both you and him) on all of your dates, then that's wrong—and you should talk to him about it. But it sounds to me like you expect him to pick up the tab for everything just because he's the guy. And that's not right, either.

Back in the old days, men paid for stuff because women generally didn't have jobs—they stayed home cooking, cleaning, and raising kids. But that changed with the women's movement, and now men and women are supposed to be equal. So you two should split everything fifty-fifty—unless you want to stay home and cook for him!

Splitting stuff doesn't have to be a hassle, either. The best way to do it is to take turns paying for things. For instance, he pays for your movie ticket and you pay for the pizza and sodas afterward. That way you both feel good about your date, and

Why not seize the pleasure at once? How often is happiness

you can concentrate on having fun together, which is what really matters.

Later,

Fiona

Vanessa <<I think that it's a problem if your guy never pays. He's not making you feel special.>>

Sirly <<Get real. You don't need a man to take care of you!>>

Who was Sadie Hawkins?

Sadie Hawkins Day, the first Saturday in November, originated from Al Capp's comic strip Li'l Abner *in the 1930s. On this day unmarried women (one who was named Sadie Hawkins) could legally chase unmarried guys, and those who were caught had to marry the women who caught them. It evolved into a dance where girls invite the guys.*

I'm dating two guys

Q. Dear Fiona,

I have been seeing two guys at the same time. Neither one of them knows about the other. I feel really bad about what I'm doing, and I know I should make up my mind about the two—but I can't. I've had so many bad relationships in the past that I want to be able to make a good decision about who I really want to be with. I think I know, but I don't know what to do about the other one. He hangs out with all of my friends, and I don't want them to think badly of me. What's my best bet?

–Confused in NJ

Fish or cut bait.

A. Hey, Confused,

There's nothing wrong with dating two guys, as long as everybody knows what's going on. That's the fair way to do it. So clue both of these guys in right away. That way there's less of a chance of anyone getting hurt.

There is a possibility that one or both of these guys may decide to give you the boot after you confess—since you haven't been totally honest with them from the beginning. But if they both decide to stick around, don't feel pressured to choose one guy right away. Take the time to figure out which one is right for you. Hey—they may both be duds, and you'll want to ditch them both!

Whatever you do, don't base your decision on what other people will think.

It's your life.

Fiona

Hiawatha ***<<I think that you should decide which guy you feel better with and stick with that one because if they find out you are two-timing, you won't have either one of them.>>***

TJ ***<<That saying–honesty is the best policy–is true.>>***

—American proverb

my best friend's ex

Q. Dear Fiona,

My best friend broke up with her boyfriend a while ago, and now he likes me. I would like to date him because I think there's a possibility we could be really good for each other, but I don't want my friend to hate me. What should I do?

—Confused in Alabama

A. Dear Confused,

Your friend may get upset. No matter how trivial or traumatic their relationship was. No matter who dumped who. No matter how long it's been since she broke up with him. No matter how completely over him she says she is. So take a step back and think about who's more important to you—someone who's been there for you through good and bad or some guy who is looking kind of cute this week.

If your best bud's the one who matters most to you, you need to be considerate of her feelings and avoid this guy. Treat your friend the way you'd like to be treated and find another guy who hasn't gone out with your friend.

Good luck,

Fiona

Do not protect yourself by a fence,

Candy <<If this girl is really your friend, she won't care. It shouldn't bother her. Remember, she broke up with him.>>

Tru <<She's your best friend. You should know if she still cares about him. And if she does, stay away!>>

Leftover <<She probably already knows you like him. Just ask her what she'd think if you guys went out.>>

Fiona says:

"Is it cool to date my best friend's ex-boyfriend?"

I get this question a lot. And in 99 percent of the cases, my answer is no. For starters, putting your love life before your friend's feelings is totally selfish. Plus it puts a strain on your friendship, and the truth is, most of the time it's not even worth it.

Good friends are forever—and guys come and go. (Sorry, but it's true.) There are tons of boys out there. Don't get mixed up with one who's already dated one of your friends. Especially if it means you'll risk losing your friendship.

I dig bad boys

Q. Dear Tucker,

I broke up with my ex-boyfriend two months ago. He had lots of problems, including a sixteen-month stay at a boot camp for being abusive to his family (he never raised a hand to me). Now I've started hanging with this other guy who was expelled from his high school and has been in trouble with the cops for grand theft auto. I see this relationship as continuing a bad trend. Do you think it's even worth a try with this new guy, or should I get out of it before I get too involved?

Thanks for the help,
–Confused

A. Dear Confused,

Sounds like you've already answered your own question, but in case you need to hear it again: Yeah, you might want to rethink where you're going with this guy.

I also think you might want to do some introspection and figure out why you keep going after bad boys. The fact that you've dated at least two guys who've been in trouble with the law says much more about you than you might realize. Do you think that good guys might be out of reach?

Of course, there's something undeniably exciting about dating

There is more to life than

people on the edge, people with a past, people that are dangerous. But you can find qualities like these in people who aren't actually criminals, and it would be smart for you to do so. Otherwise you run many risks—like ending up in trouble yourself (a 17-year-old girl in Oregon recently went to prison for two years for driving the getaway car for her bank robber boyfriend), or worrying your family, or ending up with a broken heart next time your boyfriend gets sent to boot camp or prison.

Step back and think.

Tucker

Karim ***<<You can be "bad" and a good guy at the same time. Find the guys that are on the edge—but have their priorities straight.>>***

Monica ***<<Bad boys rock!>>***

Tucker says:

I totally understand why some girls dig bad guys. It's like, by going out with someone who's considered "bad," then you get to be bad without really being bad. Bad by association. Or something like that.

Plus it's nice to see the "good" side of a bad person. You know, the artist behind the tattoos. Or the sensitive dude on the Harley-Davidson. Or the teddy bear behind the dilated pupils.

But here's the danger. When you're looking so hard for the good side in someone else, you lose track of what's most important to you: your own well-being. You gotta watch your own back.

is he too old for me?

Q. Dear Fiona,

I really need some advice. I play the piano, and I met this cute guy in my class. When I first saw him, I took him for a "bad boy" because that's what his image gave off—but he isn't. We hit it off right away, and I never thought I had a chance with him—because I'm 15, and he's in college. So I was really surprised when he asked for my number.

Ever since then we've been hanging out together. (I even snuck out of the house to see him.) But he's 22! I know this is wrong, but we both have feelings for each other. This kind of thing has never happened to me before. In one week he's met my family and learned more about me than any guy ever has in my whole, entire life. The few times I've been in his room, alone, we've ended up making out. That's all, though.

I know what you must be thinking—that he's some kind of pervert. But truthfully, he's a really nice guy. He's really smart, and I've learned a lot from him. People have been telling me that he's only trying to take advantage of me, but that's far from it. Sometimes I feel intimidated by him because he's so much older, and I think I'm not good enough for him. He's just so different. What should I do?

–M. A.

A. Hey, M. A.,

I don't doubt that this guy you're crushing on is nice (and not a pervert), but I don't think he's necessarily the right one for you. It's cool that you guys have a physical attraction and your piano

If you refuse to be made straight when you are green, you will

lessons in common—but what else is there? As you say, he's just so different. And there isn't a whole lot you can do about that. As mature as you may be, I have to tell you, you two are worlds apart. You're 15, so I'm guessing you're a high school sophomore, and he's 22, so he's probably a senior in college. Seven years is a sizable difference between any two ages—but the difference between someone in high school and a person in college is huge. While he's thinking about getting a job and starting an independent life, you're dealing with getting your learner's permit.

not be made straight when you are dry. —African proverb

No wonder you feel intimidated and "not good enough for him." And that's not how you're supposed to feel in a solid relationship—you should feel like equals. To be honest, I think a lot of guys (no matter how sweet they seem) get involved with younger girls so they can feel powerful and in control. That's weird. And wrong.

My advice? Stop hooking up with this guy! I know that ending things sounds like the end of the world, but it isn't. Maybe once you two have cooled things down a bit, you can be friends, but romantically—and I feel really strongly about this—you guys aren't right for each other.

Peace,

Fiona

In control <<He just thinks you're stupid and that he can get some from you.>>

Lioness <<Hold on to that friendship, and if he's good, he'll wait for you to grow up.>>

Joni <<This guy sounds like a loser if he can't get a girl his own age, so don't be so impressed with him. He has problems you don't want to stick around and find out about. Stop seeing him.>>

We've got this gift of love, but love is like a precious plant. You've

I blew him off, and now I want him back

Q. Dear Tucker,

I was friends with a guy named Ben, who is really great but sort of chubby. I let this whole not-perfect thing bother me for a while, and I didn't hook up with him, even though I started to really like him. And now he has a girlfriend. Do you think I could compete with her, considering he liked me for a while before she ever showed up? This sucks. What should I do?

Thanks,

–Kelly

A. Dear Kelly,

Sorry. It's normal to want what you can't have, but the bad news is, it's a little late for you and Ben. He spent a good amount of time and emotional energy digging you but getting nothing back. And now he's gone and hooked up with someone else. He got over you, and he'll probably stay that way.

The good news is, you see where you went wrong. You made a mistake. Next time you won't worry so much about appearances.

Good luck!

Tucker

Ken <<I think that you're pretty shallow in the first place to let his looks interfere with what could have been a really good thing. Now he has a girlfriend and you want to compete with her. That is wack.>>

I'm black, she's white

Q. Hi, Tucker,

I'm a black guy and a freshman in high school. I have a lot of friends, and I'm now starting to have feelings for a girl, but she's white. I don't know if I should tell her or not because I'm afraid she might not like me. And even if we did have a relationship, I don't know if my parents or her parents would approve of it. Please help me!

–Anonymous

A. Hi, Anonymous,

So, you've discovered that dating can be scary.

Yup, asking someone out involves taking a risk. The big, ugly monster we call rejection might be lurking within that cute girl you're scoping. Or not. But here's the thing (and this goes for everyone). If you don't give it a shot, you'll never know.

Now, to be fair, your risk is even greater than most. There's a lot of misunderstanding going on in this world when it comes to romance across racial lines. Which sucks. But it is a reality, and you're smart to be aware of it. Still, you have a choice: let that stuff get in the way of your life or not.

Not knowing the people involved, I can't guess how everyone will react. But I can, and do, encourage you to go for it, one step at a time. I mean, why not? We're not talking about getting married here, just a possible date. Find out if you like each other first and worry about facing the world (and your parents!) later.

Good luck,

Tucker

By the time I had reached my twenties, I had fought many battles,

Cookie *<<I've seen black guys act like they're something because they got a white girl, and that pisses me off. But if you truly like this girl, I don't think race matters. My mom is black and my dad is white and I love being mixed. Why should the color of your skin mean anything? People are people.>>*

Louise *<<My white best friend Kris has been dating her boyfriend who's black for over seven months. At first they took sh— from racists, but after all that they are still together. I would kill for what they have.>>*

Crossing the Lines

- *About half of dating teens say they've dated someone from a family much wealthier than theirs. A third have dated someone from a much poorer family.*
- *Of teens who've dated, 57 percent say they've dated people of another race or ethnic background.*
- *More than 70 percent of black and white teens said that interracial dating was "no big deal."*

Here's a story from one of our friends

I always knew Dave had a crush on me, but I wasn't interested. Not because he was black—I'm mixed, Korean and white, so interracial dating wasn't an issue for me. At least, I didn't think so. But I was infatuated with Mike—blond, blue eyes, a jock. I couldn't imagine dating anyone else.

That changed during senior year. Mike had broken my heart, and Dave and I became closer. He slipped me sweet notes in study hall that made me smile. We spent hours on the phone. He made me feel special.

When we started dating, I knew to hide it from my parents because of something my mom said. After a phone-a-thon with Dave, she snapped, "You're not dating him, are you? Because that would be a big problem for your dad and me." Problem? I mean, they were a mixed couple. They went through hell—disapproving parents, antimiscegenation [race mixing] laws—just to get married. So it never occurred to me that dating Dave would be a problem. But I got the message: I could date whites, Asians, maybe even Latinos. Just not blacks.

So I lied. About everything—where I was going, who I was with, that Dave and I were just buddies. Dave played along because he knew it was the only way we could see each other. But it made him feel bad, like a dirty secret. And that made my heart ache.

My parents weren't the only problem. Being mixed, I'd encountered racism before, but the things that happened when Dave and I were together blew my mind. Strangers mumbled, "Date your own kind," as they passed. A black waitress refused to serve us. My ex, Mike, called, yelling, "How can you kiss that nigger!" (Huh? I wasn't exactly Miss White America, yet he dated me.) Worst of all, one of my Asian friends' parents, who knew Dave and I were a couple, forbade my friend from seeing because "people might get the wrong idea about her." Suddenly it felt like the 1950s, not the PC nineties.

Dave and I hung in there for a while, but all the hostility and sneaking around took a toll on us, and after two years we broke up. We still loved each other, but it was just too hard. We both cried the day we called it quits.

Today Dave and I are still friends, and I have a good relationship with my parents—they act like it never happened. But I remember everything. And I learned three important things from the whole ordeal: love has no color; as a society, we're nowhere near Martin Luther King's dream; and if I had to, I'd do it all again. Only this time I'd fight harder.

foreign country. —Jack Kerouac

U

your relationships

Here are two big secrets to a happy relationship:

1. Communication. That means listening, too. Sure, expressing how you feel and being very clear about what's in your head is critical, but listening is even more important. Otherwise nothing ever changes. So shut up and listen. You'll hear some amazing stuff, I guarantee it.

2. Be your own person. When you're with your love object, never say, "I don't know what I want. What do you want?" You'll wind up missing all the movies you really want to see, and eating food you don't really like, and maybe forgetting about or losing a little bit of yourself. It's cool to have your own ideas, your own tastes. Be yourself—you will be loved for it.

Tucker

my friends don't like my boyfriend

Q. Hi, Tucker,

None of my friends like my boyfriend. They all think he's an annoying scumbag, and also he is really big, but I don't think that matters. He isn't a scumbag. I like him a lot, and I don't care about his weight or anything like that. I like him for who I know he is, and he's a sweetheart to me. I want my friends to like him, but all they do is make fun of me for going out with him.

What should I do?

–Michelle

A.

You sound smart—doing what you want, even if it's not the most popular thing in the world.

Look, you're always going to take a little flak from your friends about your boyfriend—no matter who he is. It's because they're jealous and want more of your time to themselves. But it sounds like you're getting hassled a little more than normal. This happened to me once, and here's what I did: I went to Taco Bell with my friends and said, straight up, "This is who I'm dating, so get over it. If you really are my friends, you will." And they did.

You can also write them a note if you feel uncomfortable talking to them about it in person. Just make it clear you're not dumping this guy, and they'll back off.

Hang in there,

Tucker

Thinking isn't agreeing or

bird <<It's kind of a sign that there may be something uncool about your boyfriend if your friends don't like him. Are you sure he's the right guy for you?>>

Floss <<If he embarrasses you in any way, he is not worth keeping.>>

my girlfriend and I never kiss

Q. Hiya, Tucker,

I'm going out with the most beautiful girl in the world, but we never talk or anything. We went out before, about a year ago, and the relationship was really rocky and we broke up. But now we're back together, and we haven't kissed or anything. What should I do?

–Joe

A. Hiya, Joe,

Dude. Kiss her today. That is, if you want to.

It sounds to me, though, that even though you call her the "most beautiful girl in the world," you're really not putting a whole lot of effort into this thing. I mean, if you wanted to talk more, you'd talk more. And if you wanted to kiss, you'd kiss.

But you aren't talking, and you aren't kissing. Are you sure you really want to be with this girl? Are you sure it's you who thinks she's the most beautiful girl in the world, or is everyone else telling you that? Did you get back together because it's comfortable and familiar or because you really want to be together?

If you want it, show it. If you don't want it, end it once and for all.

Peace.

Tucker

Tom <<Kiss her, man. She may be surprised, but she'll get into it.>>

Mari <<Are you sure she's your girlfriend?>>

You can't really call him your boyfriend if . . .

- *The only date you've had was when you sat together at the food court—with him and six of your closest friends.*
- *You've only chatted with him on-line.*
- *You've hooked up. Once. At a party.*
- *He's not sure how to spell your name right.*

my boyfriend is stressing out on me

Q. Dear Fiona,

Lately my boyfriend has been acting really edgy toward his mother and me. He seems to get annoyed with me over the littlest things, and he doesn't have any patience at all. Last night I got really upset because he told me to shut up when I asked him about his college applications.

When he realized how upset I was, he told me that there have been a lot of things annoying him lately—and he takes it out on me because he sees me the most. I don't want to ditch him—we've been together for a year and a half—I just want him to come to me with his problems instead of at me with them.

–T. G.

A. Dear T. G.,

Sounds like your guy's going through a really stressful time. The whole college application process is not only time-consuming—it's also super-high pressure. Still, your boyfriend shouldn't take his aggravation out on you.

It's normal for you to want your boyfriend to come to you in his time of stress, but it sounds like you two might actually need to spend some time apart. I'm not saying you should ditch him or anything—just give him time and space to get his head together and decompress a bit. This will also make it clear that you're not willing to let him take his moodiness out on you. You will still be

Never go to bed mad.

there for him if and when he needs you. But he'll have to ask. Nicely. Besides, he'll start missing you soon enough.

Cheers,

Fiona

Colleen <<My brother does this to his girlfriend once a month, even though he's a really great guy and he loves her. It's just that sometimes he gets real stressed out about school and sports and he gets impatient and moody.>>

Mariah <<He's probably taking it out on you because he's not that interested in the whole relationship anymore and you annoy him. Break up with him.>>

my boyfriend wants space

Q. Tucker–

My boyfriend's father died a year ago this week. The other day he told me he needed a week or two off from the relationship so he could "think about things." I asked him what those things were, but he said he didn't want to talk about it. So yesterday I saw him in the morning and told him that I really wanted to get things resolved between us, and he just yelled at me and stormed out of the room. I understand that he needs some space and that he doesn't want to be interrogated, but I feel like I should be doing more. What should I do?

–Anxious

A. Anxious–

It's hard to see someone in pain and not be able to help. You want to reach out and make a difference, but he may not let you.

When anger rises,

Giving someone space is sometimes the most difficult, exhausting thing you can do for them, but it can be an incredible help. Contrary to popular belief, when someone (especially a guy) says they want some time off, they usually really mean it. If you don't back off, if you keep trying to confront him and clear it all up, he'll start resenting you. Eventually it will spiral out of control, and there will be no hope at all. Don't fall into that trap.

To sit, wait, and not know what'll happen can be incredibly tough. But that's the best thing you can do for him right now. Eventually he'll even thank you for it.

Hang in there,

Tucker

Fiona says:

Once upon a time, I was dating this really cool, sweet guy. But he called me almost every day and wanted to chat for hours. And he also wanted to spend tons of time with me. Sounds great, right? Wrong.

See, at the time I was at a point in my life when a lot of major stuff was going down. I'd recently finished college. I'd moved out of my parents' house. I'd just started a new job that I loved. I had a lot on my mind.

So much that dating this guy got to be a drag. I began to resent him calling me. Every time the phone rang, it was like he was taking away time that I needed to myself. Eventually I broke up with him. I basically blew him off, hoping he'd just magically disappear and that I'd have one less thing to worry about. Mean, I know.

But my point is, if you don't give someone their space, they'll want it. And they'll need it. Whether you like it or not.

my boyfriend is a druggie

Q. Dear Fiona,

I recently started dating a total sweetie. But he's also a major druggie. He smokes and does every drug imaginable. I told him that as long as I never saw or smelled it on him, it was fine. But occasionally he "forgets." I really like him. We were best friends for almost two years when we decided to try being more than friends. I'm afraid that if we break up, I'll lose my boyfriend and my best friend.

Another thing—he never tries to do anything with me. I think it's because we were friends for so long, but I'm not sure. He has never even tried to hold my hand! Maybe he doesn't like me—I don't know. Please tell me what you think.

–Confused

A. Dear Confused,

Gee, what a great boyfriend. He says he wants to be with you, yet shows you absolutely no affection whatsoever. Not to say that he should be all over you or anything (that's another problem altogether), but he's never even held your hand? That's lame. What's even lamer is that he'd probably rather smoke a joint (or do whatever) than be with you, someone who obviously cares a lot about him. It's not the friendship that's keeping him from showing you love—it's the drugs.

I'll spare you the just-say-no lecture (you obviously aren't letting your boyfriend's habits affect your behavior or put your safety at risk), but just think about how he's treating you. It should kind of piss you off. Why should you settle for a pseudo-relationship when you could have the real thing with someone who's not too afraid, too apathetic, or too stoned to show some affection? It's okay to be friends with this guy, but break up with him already and find yourself a guy who will treat you with the love and respect you deserve.

It's not you, it's him.

Fiona

Sad <<Hon, if you have any respect for yourself, you would get out of this relationship. Why would you want to be with that kind of guy?>>

Grace <<How do you know he's a real sweetie if he's always messed up? Doing drugs is a way of coping with life, and they completely change your personality. You don't even know this guy.>>

For alcohol and drug abuse help lines see p. 170.

the L word

Q. Tucker,

I'd been seeing this guy for a while, and not too long ago he broke up with me. He told me the reason was because I didn't tell him I loved him! I don't think that it's right to tell someone I love them when I don't. But does it really matter that much to guys?

Thanks,

–yours always

A. Hey, yours,

You did the right thing.

You should never, and I mean never, say "I love you" to anyone unless you really mean it. That goes for everyone reading this. Love is a heavy word. It means commitment. It means sharing yourself. It mean caring deeply. Love is complicated and scary and serious and important. Are you ready to dive into all that without really thinking about what you're saying?

If you are in love with each other, then yes, hearing it is definitely important to guys. Even though they may not act like it, guys can be just as mushy as girls. They want to hear that you care, they want to feel like you're as into the relationship as they are, and if it's love, they want to hear that, too. Absolutely.

I love co-ed rock. I think it's

(Not every two minutes, please. Once in a while is fine!)

But you should never toss around the L word unless you really, really mean it. Got it?

Tucker

MeMeMe <<Tell him you love him. He probably doesn't really love you, either.>>

Marilyn: <<He's an ass. No guy who loved a girl would dump her for that.>>

you know it's serious when . . .

1. *You automatically check his horoscope when you read yours.*
2. *Things that gross you out when your little brother does them—like chew with his mouth open—make you laugh when he does them.*
3. *He's seen you caked in zit medicine, sporting baggy sweats, and with greasy hair and still thinks you're hot.*
4. *You've even stopped flirting with your best friend's hot older brother.*
5. *You can't bring yourself to delete any of his e-mails.*
6. *You do something you totally hate (like watch WWF) because he loves it, and he does something he hates (like go shoe shopping) because he knows you love it.*
7. *You don't mind that his goatee (which took three months to grow) gives you beard burn.*
8. *You've had at least one major scream-until-you're-both-crying fight, but everything was all better an hour later.*
9. *You know weird things about each other (he still has nightmares about flying monkeys from* The Wizard of Oz; *you like to smell your feet), yet you're not the least bit turned off.*
10. *You have stupid nicknames for each other that you'd rather die than say in public.*

part of the solution. —Louise Post of Veruca Salt

mr. jealousy

Q. Dear Fiona,

There's this guy I've known for seven years, and he's my best friend, but for some reason my boyfriend is jealous of the time I spend with him. They used to be really good friends—but my boyfriend has started threatening my friend because he thinks he's hitting on me.

I've tried to talk to my boyfriend about it, but he won't listen. I really care about my boyfriend and so does my friend—but he's scared of what he might do if my boyfriend doesn't get off his back. Am I missing something? Please help.

–Smile n' Nod

A. Dear Smile n' Nod,

You could literally spend hours trying to reassure your boyfriend that there's nothing going on with you and your guy friend. But that wouldn't be much fun, now, would it? And chances are, Mr. Jealousy still wouldn't believe that this dude doesn't have the hots for you. See, he's so into you that he can't imagine anyone else being able to resist your charms. Still, he's acting like an idiot, and you need to call him on that. Remind him—just once more—that it's him you like and not the other guy (and tell him you'll kick his butt if he keeps threatening your friend).

Then have a little chat with your pal, who seems to be a little more levelheaded than your man. (Jealousy can really mess with your head, after all.) Tell him that you know your boyfriend's been a little psycho lately, and ask him to hang out with you and your boyfriend a couple of times. When your

O! beware my lord, of jealousy; it is the green-ey'd monster which boyfriend sees for himself that your relationship is purely platonic, he'll realize he has no reason to be insecure or jealous, and he'll back off. If he doesn't—or if he gets violent with you or your friend—get out of there.

Peace,

Fiona

Tucker says:

Here's one important thing I've noticed about jealousy: It always passes. Whatever you get jealous about starts to seem less important day by day until you're all, "I seriously cannot believe I was so worked up about that loser." I know you've been there.

Les <<Your boyfriend sounds like a jerk. Everyone has girl friends and guy friends. If he doesn't like it, break up with him.>>

my ex is ba-a-ack

Q. Tucker,

My ex has recently showed up in my life. He wants me to come see him, but my new guy says he'll be pissed if I do. I've been with my new boyfriend over a year and a half. He says that he'll be angry even if I go where other people will see me and my ex together. Should I go out with my ex and not tell him? Or should I obey his requests?
Please help me!

–Seriously stressed!

A. Seriously,

Sounds like a problem.

Sometimes it's important to maintain a relationship with your exes—with some distance, of course. After all, you were very close for quite a while. You can't ignore that—and neither can your current boyfriend.

Obviously you're not going to start something up with your ex (right?). So where's the harm? Still, your boyfriend is clearly a little insecure about the situation, and that's understandable. But as long as you haven't really given him any major reason to think you're about to hook up with your ex, he should get over it. He shouldn't ever be allowed to control your life, or make threats, or anything like that.

If your boyfriend is still worried, make it clear (again) that nothing is going to happen. Put a (short) time limit—say, lunch at a restaurant—on how long you'll hang with your ex. And if possible, invite your boyfriend. Introduce them to each other so there's no mystery. Don't sneak around—you will get busted. And

When angry, count four;

don't fool around with your ex, you have a new boyfriend now—remember?!

Good luck.

Tucker

Tamara <<I know it's hard, but let's face it—the past is the past. Move on! You got a new man now who seems to really care for you. Why mess that up?>>

June <<I'm sorry, but you should be able to do what you want. I don't care if you have been with this guy for a month or a year—he has no right telling you who you are or are not allowed to see.>>

Fiona says:

I probably shouldn't admit this, but I'm a totally jealous person. Usually it kicks in when I'm seeing someone and they say something that makes me feel insecure. Like when my boyfriend mentions that one of my girlfriends is cute. Growl. Or when some girl starts heavily flirting with my guy at a party—right in front of me. Hiss. Whenever it happens, I'm overcome by this irrational, territorial feeling.

Experience has taught me that jealousy is ugly and it makes you do unreasonable things. Like hold a grudge against the girl at that party—or not allow your boyfriend within five hundred feet of your cute friend. And if everything is cool in your relationship, you have no reason to feel insecure in the first place.

So, beware the green-eyed monster. It is not your friend.

my ex hits me

Q. Dear Fiona,

I have this problem with my ex-boyfriend. He dated this girl for nine months, and then they broke up. I gave him time to get over her, and then he completely fell for me. We had a pretty good relationship for about a month, and then she came back into the picture. He broke up with me for her.

Since then we've broken up and gone out again five more times. The last time it got really bad—he was hitting me and everything. I don't want a relationship with a boy that hurts me, but I have feelings for him and I want to try to help him. He wants to try to work things out, but I'm scared. What if he hits me again?

—Anonymous

A. Dear Anonymous,

Do not give this guy another opportunity to hurt you again. You should never, ever stay with a guy who hits you. You might think you can change his behavior, but the bottom line is that you can't.

I know you still have feelings for him, but you must realize that you have to get over them—fast. No matter what he says, this guy doesn't love you. If he did, he wouldn't dream of raising a hand to you. Ever. The sooner you get rid of him, the better.

For your own personal safety, it's important that you talk to an adult you trust about this. Like your parents or your school counselor. They can make sure you get the help—and the protection—you need. Because this guy may freak out on you, and you

114 Maybe the most you can expect from a relationship that goes bad

could be in serious danger.

Remember, if you are ever in an emergency situation, call 911. Don't give your ex another chance. He doesn't deserve it. He hit you. And that's a crime.

Stay strong,

Fiona

Kahlua <<Do not give this guy another chance–if he hits you once, he'll hit you again. My ex used to hit me, and whenever I tried to leave him, he'd get all mushy and say he was sorry. When I took him back, he just ended up hitting me again. I finally wised up to him and left him for good and got a restraining order against him. I will never let a guy hurt me again.>>

Tiger <<Hey, this is from a guy. And what I have to say is this. For a guy to hurt a girl is one of the worst and most cowardly acts anyone can do.>>

Tucker says:

No one knows how many teens suffer abuse at the hands of their boyfriends or their parents or anyone else in their lives. But thousands of teens are being abused. Are you one of them? Chances are, if you have to think about this question for more than one second flat, you might be. Get help now. You can make things better.

For abuse help lines, see p. 170.

January
S M T W R F S
respect your emotions
the pill
take your time
condoms
communicate
protection from s.t.d.'s

your sex life

People are going to have sex when they want to. But too many people have sex when they don't want to. They make choices they aren't happy with, do things they aren't proud of, and let themselves be taken advantage of way more than they should.

It's all about control and communication.

I mean, my body is mine, right? I control it. I can do whatever I want with it. It's my decision.

And your body is yours, right? You control it. My body, my call. Your body, your call. But we can never, ever make the call for each other. Instead, we need to talk about it. We need to agree. We need to understand each other. We need to trust each other.

Instead, we need to open our mouths before we open our zippers.

Tucker

Tucker and I don't always see eye to eye. Especially about the issue of sex. But that's cool. After all, he's looking at things from the guy's point of view, and I represent the ladies. Which is why in the next section you're going to hear from us both on every issue.

See, sex is a totally different experience for young women and guys. While guys may have sex with someone for pure physical enjoyment or experimentation, girls often—but not always—want something more. Something emotional.

And depending on the circumstances, sex can either be a truly amazing experience or a completely traumatic one. The key—for both guys and girls—is figuring out where you are emotionally in the relationship before getting sexually involved.

A lot of times that means waiting—not just jumping into a sexual relationship to try to hold on to someone or because you feel like you're the last living virgin on Earth. It also means talking to the person you're with about whether or not you both feel ready to have sex. Some things are worth waiting for.

Fiona

all of my friends have done it. should I?

Q. Dear Fiona and Tucker,

I'm 16 and a virgin. Most girls my age have had sex already, and I have had a boyfriend for two weeks. I want to have sex with him, but I don't know if it's too soon—and if it is, when would it be the right time?

Should I wait until I really want to and feel that I'm ready?

–Blair

A. Hey, Blair,

First of all, I'm not going to tell you not to do it.

I am going to tell you that there are all kinds of bad reasons to do it. Right at the top of that list is the notion that everyone else has already done it. That's a lame reason. You're not living anyone else's life but your own, know what I mean? It's that whole if-everyone-else-jumped-off-a-cliff-would-you-jump? thing. Deciding whether or not to have sex is a personal decision, not a group one. Remember that—it's your decision.

Oh, and by the way, what does your boyfriend say about this whole thing? I mean, it takes both of you to do the deed. And who knows, maybe he's not ready!

If you do decide to do it, do it safely. Condoms—that is an order.

Tucker

A. Dear Blair,

I disagree with Tucker. I say, absolutely do not do it. At least not now, anyway.

You may think that you're ready for sex and that your boyfriend's really special and all—but the truth is, after going out for two weeks, you don't really know him that well. And you don't really know how you feel about him, either.

'Cause, see, you guys are in the "honeymoon" stage of your relationship. You just started going out, so you're both trying really, really hard to make things work out. He's wearing his contact lenses. You're sporting lipstick. You're both trying to be ultracool and considerate. In other words, you're not completely being yourselves. You're being your best selves.

And although you may be so into your guy's best self, what if his real self has totally nasty table manners? Or is an insensitive player who just wants some? That would seriously s-u-c-k! The best way to avoid that post-honeymoon disappointment is to take things slowly. Chill out for a bit and see how you really feel about him—you know, after things settle down a bit and he's wearing his glasses, so to speak.

Sex is more exciting on the screen and

Remember, what your friends do sexually has nothing to do with you. So stop thinking about them, and start thinking about yourself. That way you're less likely to end up doing something you'll regret.

Later,

Fiona

Ruby2000 <<Don't have sex for curiosity. Do it for love!!!>>

Lili <<If you're not 100 percent sure that you're ready, then you're not ready!>>

November Rain <<I dated this one guy for six months and we, excuse me, he decided that we needed to have sex. Stupidly, I gave in—and now, a year later, I regret everything.>>

First-Time Stats

• Twenty-four percent of girls are under age 16 when they first have sex. Sixteen percent do it at 17 or 18.

• Twenty-two percent of girls who had sex at age 15 or under say that their first experience was not voluntary.

• Only 59 percent of women and girls used contraception the first time they had sex.

Source: National Center for Health Statistics/Centers for Disease Control

between the pages than between the sheets. —Andy Warhol

am I still a virgin if . . .

Q. Dear Tucker and Fiona,

I don't want to sound stupid, but how far can you go before you technically have sex? I mean, does the guy have to be all the way inside the girl?

My boyfriend has been inside me a little bit—but not all the way. He just calls it messing around, and he's had sex before.

I don't want to have sex until I'm married, and he knows this. He has never let his stuff go when he's in. I admit I've felt a little pain when he's gone too far, but then I've stopped him.

Please tell me I'm still a virgin!

–Scared of sex

A. Dear Scared,

To be completely honest with you, I have no idea. Everyone seems to have a different definition of virgin.

But I do know this: It's what you believe that really matters. It's your virginity, not the rest of the world's. Still consider yourself a virgin? Okay, cool. It isn't anyone else's business, anyway.

Oh, and keep this in mind: If you've gone further than you want or if you feel like you're going too far just to make him feel good, check yourself. It's your body, not his.

Tucker

P.S.: Even if he's inside you just a little bit, he needs to be wearing a condom—to protect against pregnancy and STDs.

When you judge people, you have

P.P.S.: You and he won't be able to keep up this "just a little bit" thing forever, I promise you. The more you flirt with going all the way, the more likely it is that it'll happen, unexpectedly. Careful . . .

A. Hey, Scared,

I totally disagree with Tucker on this one. Dude, if it's in, it's in. And technically that means you're not a virgin anymore. No matter what your boyfriend says.

And if you ask me, it's really uncool for your boyfriend to get you to do something that you've told him you don't want to do. Especially since, I'm assuming, you guys haven't been using protection since you don't think you've been having sex. That's plain dumb.

Sorry if I sound harsh, but I think you need to be more informed about sex and about your body. Being sexually active is serious stuff. And you shouldn't be dabbling in it without knowing the facts. Asking us is a good step—find out all you can before you go any further.

Be careful,

Fiona

natalie <<Your boyfriend is disrespecting you here. You have clearly said you want to wait, and he's pushing you to do it. Stand up for yourself and say no.>>

Jewel0904 <<Physically I don't consider you a virgin, but there's no rule that says mentally you can't still be a virgin. If you want to wait so bad, don't let him get it in 'cause you are bound to go all the way and you might end up regretting it.>>

how do you get birth control?

Mom, I want to go on the pill.

Q. Dear Fiona and Tucker,

I would like to have sex with my boyfriend, but I want to be protected. He's also going to wear a condom, but I want to go on the pill just to be extra safe. My mom has offered to get me birth control because she feels that at least I'll be having safe sex. Should I talk to her (I don't really want to)—or should I go and get the birth control on my own? Can I do that?

–Wondering

A. Hey, Wondering,

It sounds like you've put a lot of thought into this, which is great. Also, your mom is really understanding. But I know that doesn't make it any easier or more comfortable asking her to get you on the pill. Talking to your parents about sex is no picnic.

But the bottom line is that if you're going to have sex, you need to be smart about it. You don't want a nasty disease. You don't want to get pregnant. So you have to do whatever you can to prevent those things from happening. Combining condoms and the pill is a good way to go.

Condoms are easy to get—you can pick 'em up at any grocery store, drugstore, family health clinic, gas station, whatever.

They're everywhere. And they're cheap, too. But to get the pill, you need to get a prescription from a doctor. And that can be trickier. You have three alternatives:

1. Tell your mom you want go on the pill, and have her take you to the gynecologist.

2. Go to your gyno, and when you're alone, ask your doctor about going on the pill. Your doctor has to keep what you discuss confidential—even from your mom. You can even ask your gyno to bill you separately for your birth control prescription so it doesn't show up on the statement your mom gets.

3. Visit a clinic like Planned Parenthood, and get birth control there. It's confidential, and in many cases you can get birth control at a discounted price since you're a teen.

Whatever you do, don't let the difficulty of getting the pill prevent you from protecting your health.

Peace,

Fiona

A. Hey, Wondering,

Fiona's already given you some great options. There are plenty of ways to get what you need without your mom. But I suggest that you let her know that you've got it covered.

Your mom wouldn't have made the offer to help you out if she didn't want to make sure that you're being safe. If you don't want to talk to her about it, find another way to let her know. Write a note or an e-mail that says, "Mom, I appreciate your offer, and I wanted to let you know that I went ahead and got everything. It's all under control. Thanks for being there for me."

It's your decision, of course, but it'd be extra cool of you to let her know you're protected. She's your mom. She loves you.

Tucker

Six Protection Options and How They Work

CONDOMS (95 to 99 percent effective against pregnancy): Latex covers the penis, and the guy ejaculates into the condom. Using them protects against pregnancy and most STDs. They're cheap and easy to find—for girls and guys. But they can break, some people are allergic to latex or the spermicide on them, and there can be a loss of sensation.

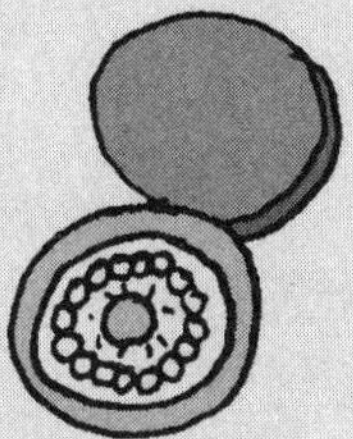

THE PILL (95 to 99.9 percent effective against pregnancy): The girl takes a pill every day, and it prevents her from getting pregnant. If taken as prescribed, it's completely effective, and there's no risk of not having anything on hand in the heat of the moment. Plus it can make your periods less painful and intense. But it doesn't stop STDs, there are potential side effects like weight gain and increased breast size, it's expensive, and you need a prescription.

FEMALE CONDOM OR SPERMICIDE (79 to 95 percent effective against pregnancy for the female condom; 72 to 94 percent for spermicide): These are over-the-counter products you insert into the vagina (follow specific package instructions). They're cheap and easy to get. But they can slip, they can cause irritation, and they're messy and hard to use.

MORNING-AFTER PILL (75 percent effective against pregnancy): If a condom breaks or you have other birth control problems, you can take this pill within forty-eight hours of having sex. It will prevent a girl from getting pregnant. But it can cause nausea, vomiting, and cramping; it doesn't protect against STDs; and you need to go to a doctor or a nearby clinic to get it (quickly).

OUTERCOURSE (100 percent effective against pregnancy): Do everything but have actual sex. This decreases the risk of STDs and nixes the risk of pregnancy. It requires restraint on both sides, and there's still a slight chance of catching STDs.

DIAPHRAGM (80-94 percent effective against pregnancy): A dome-shaped rubber cup with a flexible rim is coated with spermicide and inserted into the vagina to prevent pregnancy. It can be inserted up to six hours before sex, and can be left in for 24 hours. It can be used twice in one night without being removed (as long as you reapply spermicide). The downside is it can be difficult to insert. Plus, it doesn't protect effectively against STDs, and if you leave it in too long, you can develop toxic shock syndrome. You have to keep it in for six hours after sex (then wash it thoroughly). You must see a doctor to be fitted for a diaphragm.

Note: There is no 100 percent surefire way of protecting against pregnancy and STDs. The safest option is to double up—use a condom and the pill. And if you or your partner suspects you might be at risk for STDs, by all means get tested! Trust your instincts and use your head.

how can I hide my erections?

Q. Hey, Fiona and Tucker,

I'm a 16-year-old guy, and I get erections at the most inappropriate times. I only have to pass my girlfriend in the hall and it leaps up. I'm kind of scared someone will notice. What can I do?

–Anonymous

A. Hey, Anonymous,

Hmmm, you can always get a really big binder notebook and hide behind that. No, seriously, being a girl and all, I honestly have no idea what guys do to deal with spontaneous erections. All yours, Tucker . . .

Fiona

A. Hey, Anonymous,

Okay, first of all, sprouting woodies at the drop of a hat is completely normal. Spontaneous erections happen, well . . . spontaneously, and they happen all the time. It's just how it goes. At school, in front of the TV, while you're asleep, in church, at the grocery store, during soccer practice, wherever. They're not always tied to sexual feelings, either. . . . Sometimes it's like you blink, and whomp! there it is.

Fiona's not that far off the mark with the big binder notebook thing because there's really nothing you can do to stop yourself from getting them. It's all about hiding them.

Try tighty whiteys instead of boxers, and readjust yourself (subtly, please) when you need to. Jockey shorts tend to keep everything in place and close to the bone (excuse the pun). Don't bother trying to talk yourself out of getting erections or anything like that. It won't work. Just know that every erection is temporary, and it'll disappear as quickly as it popped up.

Peace,

Tucker

Princess2000 <<It's not a big deal. My boyfriend gets them hugging me and sometimes just talking to me. I think that it's incredibly sexy and you shouldn't be embarrassed about it.>>

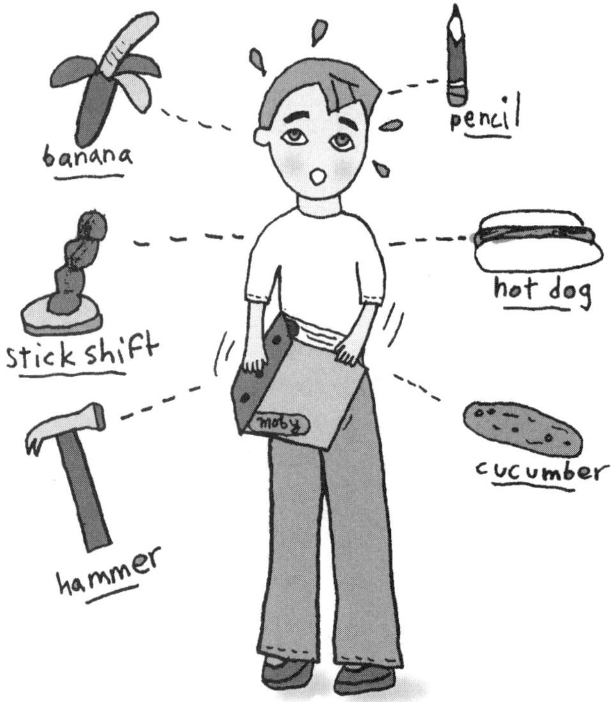

he just wants action

Q. Dear Tucker and Fiona,

I really like this guy, and he likes me, too. He invited me over to his house to watch some movies. After we got physical, he kept trying to pressure me to go further. Now I feel like he only wants me for my body or to get some "action." And now I'm afraid to go places alone with him because I think that he might make me go further than I want. But I still think I like him. Any ideas?

–Mixed Feelings

A. Dear Mixed,

We got problems. Ninety-nine times out of a hundred, if you (or anyone) are afraid to be alone with someone because you're afraid he's going to try to make you go further than you want, you're probably right. He may not attack you, but you're definitely picking up on some bad vibes . . . vibes you want to avoid.

Not all guys are like that. Although guys are generally horny and would like to get as much "action" as possible, most guys don't try to pressure girls into doing things they're uncomfortable with. I suggest you find yourself one of those guys.

From your letter, it sounds like you're kind of over this guy, anyway. You wrote: "I still think I like him." I'm not convinced. Listen to your instinct, and break this one off.

Peace,

Tucker

No one can make you feel

A. Hey, M. F.,

Break it off—now.

I know that's totally hard to do since you like this guy—and you've probably been crushing on him awhile and building him up. But he really isn't worth your time. If he truly cared about you, he wouldn't want to ruin his chances with you by putting on the pressure.

Stop seeing him before you let him talk you into doing something you don't want to do. 'Cause if you give in, you'll only end up regretting it.

Don't go along with what he wants. Go after what you want. Find someone who genuinely likes you and who won't take advantage of your feelings.

And don't feel bad—he's the one who's missing out!

Fiona

Minerva <<That women's intuition thing is a real lifesaver. Meaning if you pick up bad vibes from someone, be alert and stay away.>>

dj diva <<You should dump him! I hate guys who only want sex!! They're such pigs!!!>>

inferior without your consent. —Eleanor Roosevelt

how can you tell if someone has an STD?

Q. Dear Tucker and Fiona,

My boyfriend and I haven't had sex yet—and I think he's healthy—but I was wondering, is there any way you can tell if someone has an STD without them taking some kind of test? How?

Thanks,

–Trish

A. Hey, Trish

Nope.

Sure, some STDs have symptoms you can see, but they don't show symptoms all the time. And most STDs have no visible signs at all. Like HIV.

Sorry, but there isn't any way of knowing if he or you have an STD without being tested. Oh, and test or no test, make sure your boyfriend wears a condom. Because the thing is, there's really no such thing as a completely clean bill of health unless you get tested, then go six months

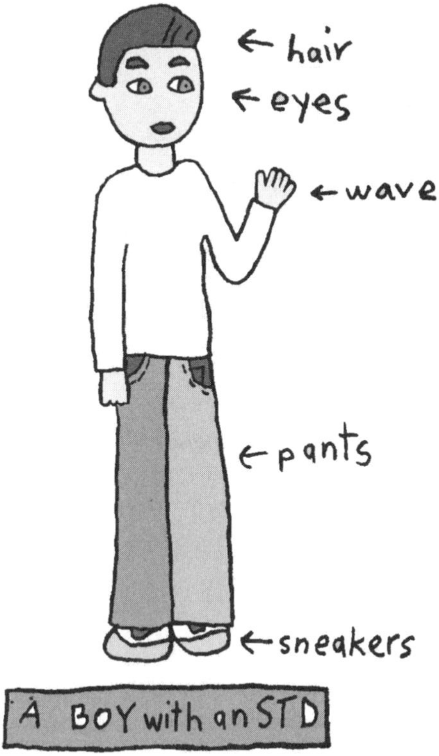

with no sexual activity at all and get tested again. And even then there's room for mistakes.

No way around it,

Tucker

A. Although some sexually transmitted diseases (like syphilis, herpes, and genital warts) sometimes have symptoms that you can see—like sores or warts on or near the genitals or an unusual discharge—the majority of STDs don't. So there is absolutely no way of knowing if you or the person you're having sex with is clean—aside from getting tested.

Even getting tested isn't 100 percent foolproof. That's why the best way to protect yourself is to use a condom every single time you have sex.

Remember: No sex is worth getting a terrible, possibly permanent disease over.

Be smart. Be safe,

Fiona

RuRu <<My advice is to wrap before you stick it! He may not want to, but you can do it for him!>>

Buddha Babe <<I have been with my boyfriend for over a year and we still haven't had sex. If you trust the guy, ask him to get tested—it can't hurt. If he won't, he's not worth doing it with. It's a trust thing.>>

for the things in which there is no doubt. —Mohammed

I'm scared I'll get HIV

Q. Hey, Tucker and Fiona,

I'm terrified. I want to have sex with my boyfriend, but I have an uncle who died from AIDS, and it was horrible. I'm really scared that I'll get HIV also. I know that people have sex all the time and they don't all get HIV, but I still can't help being scared. Help!

—Afraid

A. Dear Afraid,

I hear you. Sex can be scary business—what with pregnancy, STDs, emotional drama, etc. And HIV is the scariest of all. Luckily we know how to prevent it—condoms. If you use them, you're pretty much covered. There's no better way—except abstinence—to stay safe.

The thing about condoms is that you have to use them correctly. If you don't trust yourself or your boyfriend to be responsible and ready when and if you decide to have sex, then you shouldn't have sex yet. Don't be afraid of sex; be in control of it.

Tucker

A. Hey, Afraid,

You could literally drive yourself insane thinking about all the ways you could contract the HIV virus. But it's unhealthy to live your life in fear. Especially if there are precautions you can take that will drastically reduce your chances of contracting HIV — like knowing the person you're having sexual contact with really well and using condoms every time you have sex (oral or otherwise) and getting tested regularly.

Since there's a six month window before HIV can show up on a test, even if you're beginning a monogamous relationship and both of you test negative for HIV, you need to wait six months before doing anything that puts you at risk, then get tested again. Still, never do anything you're not ready for.

Fiona

FunGirl <<AIDS is scary. But, don't be afraid of sex. Just be careful and have fun!>>

For STD help lines, see p. 171.

The Lowdown on HIV and AIDS

What is HIV? *Contracting HIV (Human Immunodeficiency Virus) causes the onset of AIDS (Acquired Immune Deficiency Syndrome). HIV breaks down the immune system, making it increasingly difficult for the body to fight off disease. It leads to the development of numerous viral, bacterial, fungal, and parasitic infections, as well as various cancers, and usually results in death.*

How It's Spread: *HIV is spread through the transmission of body fluids such as blood, semen, or vaginal fluids (usually during sex) and through breast milk. It can also be transmitted by sharing infected needles, via a blood transfusion or organ donation, or from a pregnant woman to her baby.*

Treatment: *There is no cure for AIDS, yet, but there are many drug therapies that have been effective for some people.*

Prevention: *The only absolute way to protect yourself from any sexually transmitted disease is to abstain from sex, but you are sexually active, use condoms. That little bit of latex could save your life.*

how do I tell my parents I'm pregnant?

Q. Dear Tucker and Fiona,

I'm 13 and pregnant. I'm so scared, but I haven't told my parents yet. Is there any easy way to tell them so they don't get hurt? And should I go see my doctor before I tell them?

Luv,

–Scared

A. Hey, Scared,

You probably should get checked out by a doctor before you tell your parents that you're pregnant. I'm assuming you've taken a home pregnancy test, but a lot of times those can be inaccurate.

If you're pregnant, your body is going through a lot—and you need to seek professional help to make sure you're okay. If you're not comfortable going to your regular doctor, get to a Planned Parenthood clinic—they offer confidential and sometimes discounted services to minors.

There is no easy way to tell your parents, but if you want their help and support, you've got to. It's gonna be hard, but you won't be alone anymore—you'll have them to help you. If you are pregnant, you'll have a lot of really difficult issues to deal with—and you'll need as much help as you can get.

Good luck,

Fiona

"Don't panic." It's the first helpful or intelligible thing anybody's said

A. Hey, Scared,

First, find out if you are pregnant. That means getting a test from a real doctor—either your own or one at a Planned Parenthood clinic. The sooner you know the truth, the sooner you'll be able to deal with it.

It's important for you to have people you trust, and people who love you, on your side. In a perfect world that would definitely be your parents. In the real world it might not be. Therefore you need to line up a few more supporters—friends, peer counselors at school, a teacher, maybe clergy (if you're involved with a church or temple or whatever)—to make things a little easier.

Tell someone who can help you, even if it isn't your parents. You've got some big choices to make, and you absolutely cannot do it alone. Reach out now. Time isn't on your side.

Good luck.

Tucker

Rush <<What about the father? He made this baby, too.>>

For teen pregnancy help lines, see p. 171.

Teen Pregnancy Stats

- *Over 95 percent of 20-year-olds say they've received some formal sex education. Only 86 percent of them say that education included birth control methods. And only 89 percent say that education included "how to say no."*
- *The birthrates for teenagers 15 through 17 years dropped 5 percent in 1998 to a record low of 30.4 per 1,000.*

Source: National Center for Health Statistics/Centers for Disease Contro

to me all day.—Douglas Adams, *A Hitchhiker's Guide to the Galaxy*

your sexual identity

Frankly, unless I'm crushing on you, I don't care how you express yourself sexually. In fact, I don't even really want to think about it.

But not everyone feels that way. It may be hard for you to accept that someone is gay, but he or she is probably having a much tougher time with it than you are. Remember that crush you had that caused you so much angst? Imagine if your crush was on someone of the same sex. Now that's angst.

Oh, and if you're tempted to harass someone for being gay, check yourself. What the hell do you care? Let everyone do their own thing. Besides, leaving them alone will give you more time to do your own thing.

Tucker

my best girlfriend is a lesbian!

Q. Hey, Tucker!

I've been best friends with this girl for a long time. My problem is that she recently told me she was gay. It wasn't a huge surprise, and it really hasn't affected our friendship much because she's cool and I'm cool and all. The only problem with this is that she has a girlfriend at school that she is pretty openly gay with and I—so conveniently—lack a boyfriend. When I talk to her in the hallways now, I can't help wondering if people think I'm gay, too, and if they do, it certainly can't be helping my status with the guys. I don't want our friendship to end over this. So my question is—am I being paranoid about the situation? How can I keep my hetero profile?

—thanx

A. Hey, thanx,

Speaking as a guy, yeah . . . I think you're being paranoid. Any guy who is worth it is smarter than that—at least slightly, I hope. (If anything, it might even intrigue them, as strange as that may sound. But anyway . . .) I totally understand your worry, though. It's like when you go somewhere with a friend who's in a really wack outfit, you kind of don't want people thinking you're with them. It's like, they're not doing anything wrong, you just don't want people to assume you're the same.

But most people are a little more enlightened than that, even most guys. Let your own personality shine through, and the

We all live with the objective of being happy;

guys will come eventually. The important thing is to hang on to your friendship and be yourself. Guys worth your time are more interested in you than who your friends are.

Tucker

Lorna <<For a little while all my friends thought I was gay. I had no problem with it. I just told everyone that even though I hang around some people that are gay, it doesn't make me gay.>>

should I come out to my friend?

Q. Dear Fiona,

Help me, please. I'm a girl, and I know that I like girls. The only problem is that I'm attracted to my best friend. I hear about this all the time, but my friend is straight. It's really bugging me, and I know that if I tell my friend how I feel, she'll not only freak out—she'll tell all my other friends, too. What do I do? I can't keep this inside me forever.

Thanks,

–Friends Forever

A. Dear Friends,

If you know that your friend is straight and very likely to freak, you definitely shouldn't tell her that you're attracted to her. It's pretty clear she's not going to reciprocate in any way, and it may wind up doing your friendship more harm than good. If I were you, I'd keep your crush on your friend quiet—it'll only mess up your relationship and quite possibly complicate things with your other friends.

However, you should talk to someone. You've got some deep stuff on your mind—and you probably shouldn't keep it bottled up inside. If you don't feel comfortable talking to your friends or your family, you may want to look for support from gay groups who offer free and anonymous information, referrals, and counseling.

The important thing to keep in mind is that even though your friend may not understand what you're going through, there

Heavy thoughts bring on physical maladies; when

are other people who will—and you should reach out to them.

Hang in there,

Fiona

Emily <<I wouldn't tell her. I'm bi, and I've had a crush on a friend of mine for a while who is also female. If you feel you must tell your friend that you're a lesbian, tell her, but keep your crush under your hat.>>

Laura <<Do what your heart tells you to. If she's a true friend, she'll accept you for who you are, not for your sexuality. I was in the same situation. My best friend confessed to me that she liked me as more than a friend, and I was cool with it.>>

my brother is gay

Q. Tucker,

This is hard for me—but here goes. My brother came to my family and told us he was gay. I have had a really hard time dealing with it because my brother and I were best friends. I'm totally not homophobic or anything. But it's hard. Then someone outside of our family asked me if he was gay, and I didn't know what to say. I didn't want to say no and make my brother think that I'm embarrassed or ashamed of him, but I didn't want to say yes and have my brother get mad that I told people. What should I have done? And how can I make myself more understanding?

< rion >

A.

Everything you're feeling right now is normal. It doesn't mean you're homophobic or anything. It's confusing as hell to have someone you know and love very much all of a sudden tell you something major about themselves. You're probably thinking you don't know your brother as well as you thought.

There are a few things you might want to do. First, have a heart-to-heart with your brother. Ask him how he knew, when he knew, whether he's afraid of being harassed, stuff like that so you can understand him a little better. Next, talk to someone who understands your situation. Almost every town has a chapter of PFLAG (Parents and Friends of Lesbians and Gays)—it's a group of people who have gays and lesbians close to them, and they can help answer your questions and address your concerns.

The worst thing you can do, for yourself and for him, is to become distant. The important thing here isn't the fact that he's gay; it's the fact that he's your brother and you love him. Hang on to that, and you'll be all right.

Good luck,

Tucker

Charmaine <<I'm Catholic, and I don't believe in homosexuality, but you need to love your brother for who he is and accept it.>>

Felicia <<I don't think you should let something like this ruin your relationship with your brother. Let him know that you still love him and will be there for him no matter what.>>

Whitney <<I think in time you'll learn to cope. My mom is gay, and it was way tough. I've learned to deal. It gets better, I promise.>>

is the worst cowardice. —Confucius

I'm crushing on a lesbian

Q. Hey, Fiona,

I'm a guy, and I'm friends with this girl who's a lesbian. I really enjoy her company, but I'm afraid that her lifestyle might get in the way of us getting together. I would like to take the relationship further—as in dating. She has always been very open with me, and I don't want to destroy that. What should I do?

–Eddie

A. Hey, Eddie,

If your friend is a lesbian, and you're a guy, I think it's pretty safe to say that the relationship isn't going to go any further than friendship. Sorry. That's just kind of the way it goes, dude. Being gay isn't a lifestyle—or a choice—it's simply what she is.

And no matter how great you are, you're not going to change that—it's not about you; it's about her. And if you try to change her, she'll resent you for it. So if you really care about this girl, I suggest you try to get over your crush and just be an amazing friend to her. Remember: Although what you two have may never be romantic, it's still really special. True friends are hard to find, and you should do whatever you can to hold on to them.

Good luck,

Fiona

Francis <<Hey, fella, this ain't Chasing Amy.>>

Is Your High School Gay-Friendly?

Here are some sad stats that show most schools aren't:

- *Ninety-seven percent of public high school students report hearing homophobic remarks from their peers.*
- *The typical high school student hears anti-gay slurs twenty-five times a day.*
- *Gay and lesbian youth are two to six times more likely to attempt suicide than other youth.*
- *Eighty percent of gay and lesbian youth report verbal abuse, forty-four percent report threats of attack, thirty-three percent report having objects thrown at them, and thirty percent report being chased or followed.*

Source: PFLAG (Parents and Friends of Lesbians and Gays)

hidden paths. —German proverb

is my friend gay?

Q. Hey, Tucker,

I'm afraid my friend might turn gay. He acts really gay sometimes, and it scares me. He swears to me he's not gay and tells me when he likes a girl, but he doesn't ever ask girls out or anything. I don't think he is gay, but it scares me when he acts like this—what do I do? I don't have anything against gay people, but if he's not gay, I don't think he should act like this.

–Scared

A. Hey, Scared,

A few things:

1. People don't "turn gay." They may accept being gay, or decide to let other people know, or come out, or whatever, but they were already gay to begin with.

2. People don't "act gay." Gay people act all different ways . . . not just the stereotype you're thinking about.

3. Finding out something major about a good friend, whether it's that

I've always wanted to be something,

they're gay or something else entirely, is always hard. But it's not the end (or beginning) of the world—it's a new piece of information, which actually doesn't affect you even 1 percent as much as it affects him. If he is gay—and that's a big *if*—your friendship will be tested, and you'll have the opportunity to prove what a good friend and compassionate human being you can be.

Good luck!

Tucker

Fiona says:

Ever had a serious crush on someone before? You get these major vibes for someone, and that's just it. You're hooked, and no one can explain it or hold it against you. That's how I see the whole homosexuality issue. I mean, how can you hold someone accountable—or think they're horrible—for who they're in love with? It just doesn't make sense. Love happens. But it doesn't happen nearly enough. So when it's right, you just have to go with it. And who anyone chooses to love is nobody's business but their own.

Lindsey <<Hey, for all of you that are still against gays, I'm bi and damn proud! I have always been attracted to girls and to guys–it was something I couldn't help–so get a life!>>

but I see now I should have been more specific. —Lily Tomlin

La la la la.
chips

your family

My family is insane. Isn't everyone's? See, the thing my family always forgets is that I'm actually a person. As in, an individual. My own person. And I'm not exactly like them; know what I mean? I believe different things. I have different tastes. I'm not their mini-them.

But I have to remind myself that they're individuals, too. They think about themselves, not just about me. They do stuff I'd never do . . . and go places I'd never go. They make choices I'd never make . . . and have judgments I'd never have . . . and adore people that I can't stand. Does that make them aliens? Nope, it makes them people.

Shocking, I know. But it's a good thing to remind yourself of this—the part about them being human—especially when they seem like they came from another planet.

Tucker

my parents act like they hate me!

Q. Dear Fiona,

I have a family problem. Ever since I turned 13 (that was two years ago), my parents haven't said one nice word to me. They say I'm a snob, which I'm not. I think they're just stereotyping teenage girls, because I consider myself a good person. I used to be close to my dad, but I haven't heard him say he loves me forever. I used to be the "good kid" in the family, but now even my brothers and sisters avoid me. I get so frustrated with my parents that I won't talk to them for days on end—and they don't even care. I need my family more than ever right now! I don't know what to do.

Thanx—

–Ex-daddy's little girl

A. Dear Ex,

You've already come to the conclusion in your head that you need your parents' love and approval. Now you need to act on it. Do whatever you can to get your relationship with your family back.

For starters, talk to them. Whether you have separate, one-on-one conversations with your parents or you schedule a family meeting with everyone, the important thing is to let them know how you're feeling. Tell them you're hurt that they think you're a snob and that you need to know that they still love you.

Then listen to what they have to say, and ask them what you can do to make things better. If there's something they say you

can do to improve the situation—whether it means spending more time with them or helping them with your sisters and brothers—do it.

And don't let your frustration with the situation make it get worse. Avoiding the problem won't make it disappear. So avoid the urge to ignore your family or to hide out in your room. You'll only alienate yourself more. And no one can afford to shut themselves out like that. So start communicating and try to work it out.

Hang in there,

Fiona

Star <<Try writing a letter instead of confronting them face-to-face. Be tactful, though. Tell them you feel exiled and you need some communication. Ask why you're being avoided. Tell them you love them. It's worth a try.>>

parental pressure

Q. Tucker,

I'm on the swim team and I swim for up to about six hours a day every day. I want to quit 'cause I'm not having fun anymore. I tell my parents that, and they just don't get it. My grades are dropping and I have no social life anymore and they expect me to be a straight-A student! Please help me.

–Sick of water

A. Sick,

Parents sometimes put so much pressure on their kids to succeed that they don't notice that their kids are actually unhappy! Hate that. They believe in you, that's why they push so hard, but sometimes they need their heads checked!

Call a family meeting. I know you've told them how you feel, but it's worth another shot. Make an appointment, then sit down and go over your concerns one by one (maybe you could write everything out first). Tell them you're not happy with the way things are. Maybe you can find a compromise—like swimming only two hours a few times a week instead of six hours every day.

If your parents don't seem to be listening, you might want to talk to your swimming coach about it or a counselor at school. But don't let it go too long.

Swimming should be tough and challenging. But it should also be fun.

Tucker

Children's talent to endure stems from their

Family Fight Facts

- *What do you fight with your parents about? According to a 1996 Gallup poll of over 500 13-17 year olds:*
- *49 percent of teens said they argue with their parents about keeping their rooms clean.*
- *35 percent of teens said they fight with their parents about school, especially grades.*
- *20 percent said they argue about the way they dress and who they hang out with.*
- *20 percent said they argue with their parents over the music they listen to—how loud, what sort, etc.*
- *20 percent said they fight about drugs and/or drinking.*
- *16 percent said they have arguments with their parents about dating.*
- *9 percent of teens fight with their parents over religious matters.*

dad's female friend

Q. Dear Fiona,

My dad always goes out on Wednesdays. When I ask him where he's going, he says, "Out!" I know where he's going—to his friend's. The only problem is that his friend is a girl. When my dad is opening his e-mail, he says, "Oh, it's from ***." When he gets a phone call, "Oh, it's ***." When we're having someone over for dinner, I say, "Let me guess—it's ***!"

The thing is, my mom is totally fine with it! Her friends are, too. It pisses me off! I told my mom how I feel and she said that I should spend time with *** and get to know her better, but I refused. My dad's friend acts like my other mom! And everyone's fine with it except me. What should I do?

–Utterly Pissed Off

A. Dear U. P. O.,

Obviously you're feeling threatened by your dad's relationship with this other woman. And that's totally normal. The well-being of your parents' marriage directly affects your life, and you have every right to wonder—and ask about—the relationship between your dad and his friend. I'd suggest that you call a meeting with everyone in your family—and clue your parents in to how you're feeling.

Most likely, your dad and this woman are just buddies. I know it's sometimes hard to grasp, but your parents are human—and just like you, they have every right to have friends of the opposite sex. I mean, think about it: You have guy and girl friends, right? Right. And that's not going to change just 'cause you grow older—or even when you get married.

If your mom knows about your dad's friendship with *** and isn't worried about it, then there's probably no need for you to be freaked out. But wouldn't you rather hear it from them than from me?

Talk to them.

Fiona

Bernie <<I had the same problem except in my case he was actually having an affair. All I can say is he's still your dad and that he does care for you. It's good that you showed your mom you care.>>

my parents' divorce is taking over my life

Q. Dear Tucker,

My mom and dad aren't together, but they live in the same town. They made some deal where I'd spend the week with my mother and the weekend with my father. Okay, fine. I like them both. But I want to spend the weekend hanging out with my friends! I feel bad blowing off my dad, but I can't really see my friends when I'm across town at his place. What am I supposed to do?

–Torn

A. Dear Torn,

I know the feeling. It's like, "Hey, guys. It's not my fault you got divorced. Why am I the one who has to suffer?" The sad fact is that when there's a divorce, everyone has to deal. Even though the situation you've worked out doesn't sound like the worst plan in the world, it's still a hassle, and it's getting in the way of your friendships. If I were you, I'd come up with a new plan. Like fewer weekends with Dad—spend some weeknights with him instead.

The thing is, raising this issue could cause all sorts of emotional drama. Your parents might get all worked up about who you're spending more time with and who you like better and all the rest of it. So to introduce your idea, I think you should write it down and give both of them a copy. Explain that you love them both, but you need to spend more time with your school friends on the weekend. Friends are important, too. On paper,

It is possible to adapt to a given hard situation precisely because you it'll seem very straightforward, and you'll have a better chance of getting your way without the tug-of-war.

Good luck,

Tucker

P.S. —If possible, make it clear that you won't have to rely on them for transportation. That was always a sticking point for me. Don't have a car? Suck it up and take the bus. It's worth it.

P.P.S. —Even though this is hard now, you'll be a more independent, self-confident person because of it, I promise. Hang in there.

Divorce bites <<Hardly anyone I know has parents who are still together. You're lucky they're both still in the same town.>>

Divorce Stats

As of 1990:

- *1.6 percent of children had parents who were divorced.*
- *16 percent were living in joint custody arrangements.*

As of 1998:

- *There were 955,000 divorces in the U.S. in 1998 alone.*
- *27.7 percent of all people under 18 lived with only one parent.*
- *85.1 percent of single-parent homes were headed up by the mother.*

Source: Department of Health and Human Services

have got to live with it every day.—Steven Biko, South African activist

my sis wants to move out!

Q. Hey, Fiona,

I'm really scared! My mom and sister had a major fight, and now my sister might go live with our dad and stepmom. I really don't want her to, but she's had a lot of problems with my mom—even stuff that happened before I was born that I don't know about! Should I step back and let everything happen or should I try to get my mom and sis to make up? I have good relationships with both of them, and they try to get me involved. What should I do?

—Anonymous

A. Hey, Anonymous,

I don't think I know a single kid who hasn't fought with their parents. But when things get to the level they're at with your mom and sister, that's serious. You have every right to be freaked out.

Let everyone involved—your mom, your sister, and your dad—know that you don't want your sister to move out. Although you might not be able to prevent it, getting your feelings off your chest can only make you feel better. Also, it seems like your mom and sister want your input and help in working things out. So do what you can to ease the tensions.

But remember: If they aren't able to reconcile, don't blame yourself. They may both need a cooling-off period before they can start communicating like people who love each other.

Take care,

Fiona

Look for the good, not the evil,

Goldie <<I just went through the exact same situation, but I'm the sister who moved out. I'm a lot happier with my dad and stepmom, but I still go back and see my brother a lot.>>

Tiny <<Tell each of them at different times how you feel. Don't yell, though. If it helps, write them each a letter and drop it on their pillow or something. They may not make up, but they'll be more considerate.>>

my bro is a f***-up!

Q. Tucker,

A couple of days ago my mom found cigarettes and chew in my brother's car. He claims that he went to a party and gave someone a ride that left them there. I really want to believe him because I look up to him a lot. But then again, I never really know what he does. It really upsets me because I want to be like him, but I don't want to smoke. He told me he'd never do it because it's gross and bad for you and it would ruin his sports, but I'm not sure whether or not to believe him.

~KC~

A. Hey, ~KC~,

You see evidence that your biggest role model is doing something very un–role modely. Bummer! I don't know whether or not he's telling the truth. But when it comes to you and your choices in life, it really shouldn't matter.

See, your brother, besides being sort of a hero to you, is just a guy. That means he isn't perfect. So what you need to do is figure out what parts of him you admire and what parts you don't and follow his example accordingly. You are your own person, not just his sibling.

I'd give him the benefit of the doubt if I were you, but more important, choose your own course.

Chin up,

Tucker

Laura <<It's just cigarettes. It's not like you walked in on your brother shooting up or anything.>>

Brandy <<Smoking doesn't have anything to do with who your brother is and whether or not you should look up to him or not. If you want to know so badly, why don't you just confront him?>>

Fiona says:

When you're living under your parents' roof, you have to live by their rules.

But that doesn't mean you have to believe everything they believe in, or act like they do, or like the same types of people, or dress like them, or like the same music, or eat the same food, or whatever.

Ultimately it's up to you what you believe, who you hang out with, and so on. Making new friends and trying new things can be a wonderful experience, as long as you don't sneak around behind your parents' backs. That's usually what upsets parents most.

You can be your own person without breaking the rules.

trouble troubles you. —American proverb

did my sister's bf hit her?

Q. Dear Tucker,

I'm worried about my big sister. I look up to her, but she's dating this guy who's kind of notorious for being a big druggie. He's even been to rehab. Last night she had a black eye. She told everyone he accidentally bumped her face with his elbow. Should I be worried?

—Wondering

A. Dear Wondering,

It's hard to say if you should be worried or not. She might be telling the truth—it really might have been an accident. Then again, it might not have been. Sometimes people who really seem to have their stuff together find themselves in bad relationships or even dangerous ones.

Dissing the guy your sister is dating won't work. It'll piss her off, even if she knows he's bad. Because when you say he's a loser, you're also saying she has bad judgment for dating him, and she doesn't want to hear that. Still, it's time to have a chat with your sister. Tell her that you look up to her and that no matter what you do, you can't help feeling that this guy is no good. Let her explain. Maybe she'll put your mind at ease.

Start getting really worried if and when you start to see a pattern. As in, more injuries. Making lame excuses for why she can't see you. Or other random behavior that freaks you out. Then and only then talk to someone you can trust—a parent, counselor, teacher, older friend, clergy, whatever. Or check out your yellow pages for domestic crisis centers or abuse hot lines.

Don't jump to conclusions, but keep your eye on things. Your

Distrust interested advice.

sister's lucky that you are there for her no matter what.

Tucker

P.S. Fingers crossed—maybe he came out of rehab a new person. People who've gone through drug problems always deserve a second chance.

my parents snoop!

Q. Dear Fiona,

I've got this huge problem that just drives me crazy. My parents are so nosy. I mean, they don't seem to understand the word privacy. They listen in on my phone calls, read my e-mails, snoop in my room looking at everything, and sometimes even take stuff from my room and don't give it back!

I mean, I have nothing to hide, but what's their problem? They have no right to go into my room and look at my things. They have no right to listen in on my conversations with my friends. A girl's got to have some freedom in her life.

What should I do to stop my parents from being so nosy? I just can't take it anymore.

Sincerely,

—Frustrated Teen

Love all, trust a few.

A. Hey, Frustrated Teen,

It's time to have a little chat with Mom and Dad. Obviously they're paranoid that you're up to no good. I don't know what they think you're doing, but for whatever reason, they feel like they can't trust you to tell them what's up. If you want them to stop snooping, you have to prove 'em wrong.

You say you have nothing to hide, so explain to your parents that you're not doing anything they should be concerned about. No sex. No drugs. No cults. Whatever. Then ask them to trust you enough to respect your privacy—and your property.

And if you really want them to stop snooping, you should try to give them just enough info to get them off your back (or out of your diary).

Unfortunately, there's a chance that this won't work. No matter how much their kids tell 'em, some parents feel that the only way they can keep tabs on them is through surveillance. If that's the case, then you'd better be aware that your parents are probably still spying on you and act accordingly.

Good luck,

Fiona

Rosa <<My parents are exactly like that. They do just about everything. My life is open to everyone since I have no privacy. My dad goes through my floppy discs to see if I have any guy pics. When he sees them, he erases them.>>

Jennifer <<I think you should tell your parents straight up, "Hey, I need some privacy." And if that doesn't work, tell them it really ticks you off!>>

–Shakespeare, *All's Well That Ends Well*

Sign-off

We hope we hit you up with some useful things to think about. That's our job as advice people—not to solve problems, really, but to give you another point of view (or two) so you can make your own choices.

Think about it. Who knows your situation better than you do? No one. (Not even us.) In the end, you have to make your own decisions. Good ones, we hope.

Unfortunately, every once in a while you're bound to screw up and make a bad decision. Just like everyone else on the planet. But the more it happens, the more you realize mistakes aren't the end of the world (even if it feels that way at the time). You'll get past the rotten decisions and learn from them. And next time around, you'll handle it better.

You might get so good at problem solving that you'll be the one giving advice! And you'll be prepared . . . at least to listen and maybe to pass on a few words of wisdom.

Whatever you do, be safe and stay happy.

Peace,

Tucker and Fiona

help lines

ALCOHOL AND DRUG ABUSE

National Drug and Alcohol Treatment Referral Routing Service
(800) 662-HELP

National Council on Alcoholism and Drug Dependence, Inc. (NCADD)
(800) 622-2255
www.ncadd.org

Al-Anon/Alteen Family Group Headquarters, Inc.
(800) 344-2666 (U.S.)
(800) 443-4525 (Canada)

Narcotics Anonymous
(818) 773-9999
www.na.org

White House Office of National Drug Control Policy
www.freevibe.com

ANOREXIA AND BULIMIA

The American Anorexia/Bulimia Association at (212) 575-6200. Call for referrals in your area.
www.aabainc.com

The Remuda Ranch Centers
(800) 445-1906

DEPRESSION, SUICIDE, AND RUNAWAYS

Covenant House National Hotline (for Suicide and Runaways)
(800) 999-9999

National Runaway Hot Line
(800) 621-4000
www.nrscrisisline.org

Children of the Night
(800) 551-1300
www.childrenofthenight.org

Depression and Cutting Yourself (Self-Injury) Information Hot Line
(800) DONT-CUT

GAY AND LESBIAN

The National Youth Advocacy Coalition (NYAC)
www.nyacyouth.org
Or e-mail them at nyac@nyacyouth.org for info and referrals to local groups.

The Gay and Lesbian National Hot Line
Toll-free, anonymous counseling, referrals, and information
(888) THE-GLNH

The National Hot Line for Gay, Lesbian, and Bisexual Youth
(800) 347-TEEN

Parents and Friends of Lesbians and Gays (PFLAG)
www.pflag.org or call PFLAG's Washington, D.C., headquarters at (202) 638-4200

RAPE, ABUSE, AND INCEST

RAINN (Rape, Abuse & Incest National Network)
(800) 656-HOPE
www.rainn.com

SOAR (Speaking Out About Rape)
www.soar99.com

National Child Abuse Hotline/ChildhelpUSA
(800) 4-a-child
www.childhelpusa.org
National Domestic Violence Hotline
(800) 799-SAFE
www.ndvh.org

SEX, STDS, AND PREGNANCY

Planned Parenthood
(800) 230-plan
www.plannedparenthood.org
special teen site:
www.teenwire.com/index.asp

America's Crisis Pregnancy Helpline
www.thehelpline.org
(888) 4-options

Loser boyfriends. Back-stabbing friends. Family trauma. Fiona addresses all those problems and more in her daily advice column on Alloy.com. This New York City chick also co-authors Alloy's sex ?s column with Tucker (but don't tell her mom that!), and writes fashion and entertainment stories and quizzes for the site, too. Because of her advice gig at Alloy, ALL of her friends ask her for advice ALL of the time. Especially her exes. But Fiona's cool with that. Most of the time, anyhow. When she's not working, she's hanging with her pals, straightening her apartment, rocking out to Pavement, and shoe-shopping. Got issues? Drop her a line: askfiona@alloy.com.

Tucker is Alloy's advice guy. Why? Well, it's not because he's written for every teen magazine you can think of (which he has, along with a bunch of grown-up ones. Not "adult" ones, just grown-up ones. Get your mind out of the gutter.) Nope, he's Alloy's advice guy because he's been through it. You name the problem, he's been there. Probably twice. And if he hasn't, he does his best to relate. Anyway, everyone asks him for advice all the time, and always has. Guess it's because he gives it to you straight, even when it's not necessarily what you want to hear. Wanna test him out? E-mail him: asktucker@alloymail.com.